Confusion exists in today's Church concerning the nature, source, and use of faith. In some cases, faith seems to have become a magic lamp—rub it, and your every wish will come true! Others try to "develop" their faith, "earn" their faith, or "fake it." Here Judson Cornwall offers an authoritative, useful definition of true faith, giving comfort and guidance to the Christian perplexed by today's varying statements on the fruit and gift of faith.

BY Judson Cornwall
Let Us Abide
Let Us Enjoy Forgiveness
Let Us See Jesus
Let Us Praise
Let Us Draw Near
Let Us Be Holy
Heaven
Unfeigned Faith

Unfeigned

Faith

Judson Cornwall

Power Books

Fleming H. Revell Company
Old Tappan, New Jersey

Library of Congress Cataloging in Publication Data

Cornwall, Judson.
    Unfeigned faith.

    1. Faith. I. Title.
BV4637.C64   234'.2   81-762
ISBN 0-8007-5057-8   AACR2

To Dr. Fuschia Pickett,
a longtime friend, a capable teacher of truth,
a scholar in the Scriptures, and a colleague in the ministry.
Her life of faith has been an inspiration to multitudes.

Acknowledgments

When the Fleming H. Revell representative phoned, asking me to drop everything that I was doing to write a book on faith, I declined because of a heavy conference schedule. He was persistent, though, and after prayer I consented. I wrote this book while traveling in excess of 25,000 miles, using every minute that could be taken from another activity. In order to meet the deadline that was set, I needed help, and it was made available most graciously.

I want to thank my wife, Eleanor Cornwall, for being a sounding board by reading the first drafts and offering her criticisms and comments, and for checking all Scripture references.

My thanks, also, to my capable secretary, Cheryl Tipon, for giving priority to editing my final drafts for spelling, punctuation, grammar, and style.

Thanks to Vonnie McClure, who helped me write my last book, for dropping everything she was doing to hastily type the final manuscript.

Although acknowledged elsewhere, I want to express special thanks to the Reverend Dick Mills and his staff for some in-depth research they did for me.

And heartfelt thanks be to God for a wonderful flow of His anointing during the writing of this book.

Contents

10   Contents

SECTION I

Unfeigned Faith and Its Correlatives

Prelude
Correlatives to Faith

Perhaps I will be forgiven for using terms with which organists and pastors are most familiar if I admit that I spent many years on the organ bench in churches, and I pastored for nearly thirty years. To me, *prelude, interlude,* and *postlude* are logical divisions and progressions in the development of a theme. The first indicates something is about to commence, the second prepares for a change, and the third concludes the whole.

That a prelude is necessary to a book on faith is occasioned by much confusion in the body of Christ concerning the nature, source, and use of faith. It seems that there has been such a proliferation of simplistic faith theology that the relation of faith to the whole counsel of God has been exaggerated, and faith itself has been deified. We hear less and less about the faith of God that comes as a result of relationship and more and more about "our" faith that can be increased and then exercised for anything our hearts desire. Faith almost becomes like Aladdin's magic lamp that, when rubbed, produced a genie whose whole purpose of existence was to fulfill the wishes of whoever rubbed the lamp and incanted the magical formula.

Unfortunately, faith is not often taught as a divine enablement that will reveal God and His kingdom to the believer; it usually is projected as an energy that can force God to obey the commands of the practitioner. Faith as I have heard it declared on the lecture platforms deifies man and humanizes God, inasmuch as man becomes the commander ("whatever you say . . .") and God becomes the complier ("God is honor bound to do . . ."). Yet the Scriptures declare that Christ Jesus is the Lord, and we are His servants; He gives the orders, and we obey. How far we have departed from the unfeigned faith that was in Timothy, his mother, and his maternal grandmother!

When Paul spoke of the *unfeigned* faith that was demonstrated in the life of Timothy (*see* 2 Timothy 1:5), he used the Greek word *anupokritos,* which is used six times in the New Testament. Four of those times it is translated "unfeigned"; once it is translated "without dissimulation" ("Let love be without dissimulation . . ." [Romans 12:9]), and once it is translated "without hypocrisy" (". . . wisdom from above is without partiality and without hypocrisy" [James 3:17]). Hence we are challenged to have unfeigned love, unfeigned faith, and unfeigned wisdom.

The Reverend Dick Mills, a word-study specialist, has long been a personal friend of mine. When I discussed this book with him, he became excited about its potentialities and immediately phoned his staff, urging them to do a computer printout on the word *unfeigned* and to research the commentaries on this verse. He sent me forty-three separate translations of 2 Timothy 1:5, in which Timothy's faith is spoken of as *unfeigned* seventeen times, *sincere* fourteen times, *genuine* four times; and then once or twice the word *anupokritos* is translated as "true faith," "trust," "unalloyed," "unhypocritical," "heartfelt," and "guileless."

When the staff checked their lexical sources, they uncovered an even greater diversity of words to express *unfeigned.* When I alphabetized them, I found these fifteen different expressions: "frank, free from insincerity, genuine, guileless, not playing a part, real, sincere, true, unassumed, undisguised, undissembled, unskilled in simulation, without pretense, without hypocrisy, and without simulation."

After joining his staff in the research, Dick Mills wrote me, "Unfeigned faith is faith without pretense, faith without a mask, without putting on an act or merely reciting dialogue as though you're reading a script."

Oscar R. Mangum said, "You can depend on a man when he has (unfeigned) sincere faith. He has a bed-rock under his feet and knows where he is going."

Section I of this book seeks to define this unfeigned faith as well as present a series of correlatives, or those terms that are regularly used in conjunction with faith. Perhaps a redefinition will result in a redirection of our faith.

1
Unfeigned Faith

While I nervously shifted my weight from one foot to the other as I waited backstage for the cue to my first entrance in the school play, the director interrupted my fearful musings to say, "Judson, relax! If you forget your lines, just fake it."

So I did.

Years later, during my college days when I was an assistant pastor in southern California, a young couple stopped by the church one afternoon, wanting to get married before the fellow was shipped overseas. I apologized that the pastor was out of town, but they merely asked me to perform the ceremony. When I explained that I had never done so before, and that I didn't even have a copy of the Protestant wedding ceremony available to me just then, the sailor confidently said, "Then just fake it."

So I did.

Time marched on, and I found myself the organist for a large camp meeting in the state of Washington. The evening soloist stopped by the organ on his way to the microphone and showed me a new piece of music, asking me to transpose the song to a lower key for his voice range. Having agreed to do so, I was surprised to discover that he had only the one sheet of music, which he took with him to the podium. When I gestured my need for the music, he merely smiled and said, "Just fake it."

So I did.

I cannot remember how many times in my ministry I have

had to improvise, depend upon my memory circuits, bluff my way through, and just plain fake it, but they are multitudinous. All of us do this; it is a part of living.

Unfortunately, we tend to carry this capacity for improvisation right into our relationship with God, and if we lack a necessary divine grace, we merely fake it. Especially does this seem to be true in the matter of faith. None of us seems willing to admit to an absence of faith, so we pretend, simulate, masquerade, counterfeit, and just plain fake it. This, of course, calls for the use of many similes for faith, and we must be prepared to rationalize away the failure that follows, but as long as it looks and sounds as though we possess faith, we seem to be content, and others seem to be satisfied.

Though it may speak well of my powers of observation that I could fake a wedding ceremony, and testify to my ear for music that I could fake an accompaniment for a song unknown to me, it can only affirm my stupidity when I pretend to have faith, for "without faith it is impossible to please him . . ." (Hebrews 11:6).

Faith is the key to our entire relationship with God. We are "saved through faith" (Ephesians 2:8), "sanctified by faith" (Acts 26:18), "justified by faith" (Galatians 2:16), and we are "kept . . . through faith" (1 Peter 1:5). All of the graces of God are entered into through the doorway of faith, for Paul wrote, "Therefore being justified by faith, we have peace with God through our Lord Jesus Christ: By whom also *we have access by faith* into this grace wherein we stand, and rejoice in hope of the glory of God" (Romans 5:1,2, italics added).

Surely, then, faking faith is far too dangerous to be worth the gamble. After God intervenes in the affairs of our lives in such a way as to produce a living faith, none of us would dare try to function without it, or even worse, try to bluff our way through when dealing with Almighty God. Or would we? If so, we wouldn't be the first to at least try it.

No nation on the face of the earth has ever been more aware of the direct intervention of God in her national affairs than Israel. Delivered from slavery and directed to the Red Sea, where God could decontaminate them from their former captors once and for all, Israel became a nation under God in a day. Faithfully God defended His people, defined His laws, demonstrated His power, and devoted Himself to supplying every physical and spiritual need among them. He designed a tabernacle for a meeting place with Himself, and He deputized Aaron as their priest and the entire tribe of Levi to assist the people in their worship. They were declared to be His people, and they submitted to complete dependence upon Him in everything.

Israel lacked nothing from the day she left Egypt to the day she entered Canaan—nothing, that is, except faith, for Deuteronomy 32:20 tells us that the Lord said, "I will hide my face from them, I will see what their end shall be: for they are a very froward generation, *children in whom is no faith*" (italics added).

Israel lacked not provision but performance of faith. The parting of the sea, the sweetening of Marah's waters, the daily manna, the guiding cloud, the smitten rock that provided continuous water, plus the voice of God were all faith producing. They were incontestable evidences of God's goodness, grace, and glory. Still, Israel murmured ten or more times, sought to return to Egypt's slavery several times, made a golden calf as a replacement for God, and secretly carried images of Egyptian gods throughout all of her wanderings.

But for all of her "frowardness" (perversity, disobedience), fear, and idolatry, Israel never admitted her lack of faith. Instead, she faked it. Tabernacle services never ceased, sacrifices were never discontinued, feast days were faithfully observed, and the cloud was dutifully followed all the days of the wilderness wanderings. The people still performed as though they had faith, but they were hypocritically pretending—theirs was a feigned faith. Is ours?

When Paul wrote to Timothy, he spoke of unfeigned faith in both letters. Interestingly enough, both times it is in chapter 1, verse 5. First he wrote, "Now the end of the commandment is charity out of a pure heart, and of a good conscience, and of *faith unfeigned*" (1 Timothy 1:5, italics added). He stated not only that faith and love are ultimates, but that the love must come from a pure heart, and the faith must be genuine—"unfeigned."

The second time Paul wrote to Timothy, he said, ". . . I call to remembrance the *unfeigned faith* that is in thee, which dwelt first in thy grandmother Lois, and thy mother Eunice; and I am persuaded that in thee also" (2 Timothy 1:5, italics added). Three successive generations possessed unfeigned faith, or as other translators have put it, "unalloyed" (Berkeley), "unqualified" (Amplified), and "unhypocritical" (Wuest).

The faith that pleases God and moves His hand on behalf of His children, then, is unfeigned faith, faith that is undisguised and without hypocrisy. Counterfeit faith is never accepted in Heaven's bank. But what is genuine faith?

W. E. Vine, in his book *An Expository Dictionary of New Testament Words,* says of the Greek word for faith, "*Pistis,* primarily a firm persuasion, a conviction based upon hearing (akin to *peitho,* to persuade), is used in the New Testament always of faith in God or Christ, or things spiritual."

Far from exhausting the meaning of the word *faith,* this merely indicates the normal usage of the Greek word.

Through the years, others have added their views to this definition. For instance, Dr. John Erskine defined faith by declaring, "It is, in general, an assent to the word of God, in which there is a light, a glory, a brightness, which believers, and they only, perceive. In particular, it is an assent of the understanding to the Gospel method of salvation; in which there is an excellency and glory which only believers see. A supernatural conviction of this is faith."

Upon hearing Dr. Erskine give this definition of faith in a sermon, John Wesley said he would wholeheartedly concur if Erksine would simply use the word *conviction* in place of the word *assent*.

If faith is, indeed, a conviction, an assent, to the word of God, which produces an inner illumination and glory peculiar to believers, then it will be very difficult to counterfeit. We may fake assent, but it is difficult to pretend divine illumination and glory.

Others have pointed out that faith always produces. Something happens when faith is released. Faith saves, faith heals, faith obeys, and faith cleanses. Faith reaches into the unseen world and brings visible evidence into the seen world. Faith is active, never passive.

When Jesus exercised faith, the fig tree dried up from its roots, bread and fish were multiplied to feed vast multitudes, blind eyes were opened, demons were cast out, and even the dead were raised. His faith was potent and productive. It was rooted in God and released to men. It calmed the storm, walked on the water, turned water into wine, and rode an untrained donkey in a parade of shouting people. Surely this was "faith unfeigned," for no one could fake these actions.

Either "Now faith is . . ." (Hebrews 11:1), or it is not. All of the right words and religious ritual can never successfully replace true faith, for faith alone accomplishes divine results.

In my book *Let Us Abide* I point out that "it is called *precious* faith (*see* 2 Peter 1:1) and *holy* faith (*see* Jude 20, italics added). Its value is priceless, and its virtue is peerless." Any attempt to fake a precious and holy faith is doomed to failure from the very start, for the crass hypocrisy behind the pretense precludes a holy result, and what could be precious and priceless about a feigned faith anyway?

Mental assent, emotional stirrings, and misdirected zeal are often substituted for true faith, but when the test comes, these expedients always fail. No matter how strong the emotions or how fervent the zeal, they never metamorphose into faith, any more than an incubated hen's egg can ever produce a calf. They are distinct and separate, and neither can be transformed into the other.

Perhaps the greatest tragedy of feigned faith is the total needlessness of it. Divine faith is abundantly available, thereby nullifying the need for spurious faith. "So then faith cometh by hearing, and hearing by the word of God" (Romans 10:17). Faith flows when God speaks, for God Himself is the source of our faith, and His quickened word is the channel through which that faith is transmitted to men. God has never been known to have a shortage of faith, but men have been known to be deficient in their hearing of the voice of God, thereby depleting their faith.

Unfeigned faith is God's ultimate for all of our lives. True, pure, holy, precious faith that is unadulterated, undisguised, unalloyed, unqualified, and without hypocrisy is God's never-changing goal for His church and every member in it.

Among the greatest reasons for feigned faith is a weak understanding of the manifold and magnificently varied facets that make up divine faith. Possibly we've tried to bake our "faith cake" with too few ingredients. If so, the cause of failure is self-evident. Success in a life of faith, just as much as in cooking, demands a proper blend of all the necessary ingredients. A prayerful consideration of the components of faith as presented in this book may very well prevent our faking faith, or equally as bad, trying desperately to produce what only God Himself can produce. Seeking to create faith will be not only frustrating but fruitless, for, of course, only God can create faith.

2
Faith Provided

Before his death in 1969, Harold Horton, that great English Bible teacher, wrote, "Faith is the normal atmosphere of Heaven so difficult to acquire on earth for the obvious and revealed reason that all Hell is against it. For by faith the weakest among us may storm the battlements of Hell and hurl the enemy from his challenging chariot."

"Faith is the normal atmosphere of Heaven...." Certainly, then, it would be an abnormal atmosphere on earth, for sin has so defiled the place of our residence that it no more resembles God's homeland than darkness resembles light. For one on earth to live in the atmosphere of heaven would require a transfusion, a transference, or a transmission of God's atmosphere into man's atmosphere. It cannot be synthesized or produced by man any more than darkness can produce light, but light can be beamed into the darkness, transforming it into brilliant brightness; and the more light, the greater the brilliance.

While man is not inactive in the production of faith, he is not the initiator of it. Faith does not have its origins in the heart of man but in the Word of God. Faith is a heavenly grace made available by God's mercy through His Word.

In my book *Let Us See Jesus,* I say:

> Faith is produced by God, not by man. Faith is a divine
> energy, not a religious one. It has its origin in the Godhead,
> not in the Body of Christ. We're not capable of producing

this dynamic of faith, only of receiving it. In the same manner that homeowners don't produce electricity, but only consume it, we do not produce faith; we only utilize it. Furthermore, the generator that produced electricity does not consume it; it transmits it. Similarly, God does not produce faith to consume it, but to transmit it. We receive faith not to learn how to produce it, but to learn how to release it.

Faith's source is in God the Father, God the Son, and God the Holy Spirit, not in the Bible, not in theology, not in doctrine, although sometimes doctrine is called "the faith." The Bible, theology and doctrine will direct faith, but will not produce it.

Faith is not even produced by prayer, fasting or works, though these might release faith. Fasting for faith might produce a weight loss, and working for faith may bring about exhaustion, but faith is not produced by man's efforts; its source is totally in God. "God has dealt to every man the measure of faith" (Romans 12:3).

Paul teaches this most authoritatively in the tenth chapter of Romans, which some see as a parenthesis in the book in which he communicates his deep desire that Israel might be saved. He points to Israel's zeal but declares that they seek to establish their own righteousness without accepting God's provision of righteousness, Jesus Christ. This righteousness, Paul declares, comes by faith (*see* v. 6), and assures them, and us, that ". . . The word is nigh thee, even in thy mouth, and in thy heart; that is, the word of faith, which we preach" (Romans 10:8).

Immediately after establishing that ". . . whosoever shall call upon the name of the Lord shall be saved" (Romans 10:13), Paul begins to ask, "How then shall they call on Him in whom they have not believed? and how shall they believe in him of whom they have not heard? and how shall they hear without a preacher? And how shall they preach except they be sent? . . ." (Romans 10:14, 15), and then declares, "So then faith cometh by hearing, and hearing by the word of God" (Romans 10:17).

The Greek word Paul uses here for "the Word of God" is *rhema,* which emphasizes the speaking of the word rather than the word that is spoken. While God is talking, while the speaking is going on, faith is being transmitted; faith is coming via the voice channel of God. Divine energy accompanies God's voice, and the Bible calls that energy "faith." This is consistent with the context of Paul's message in this chapter, for he has been most concerned that the message of Christ be declared, preached, and proclaimed to his own countrymen, since ". . . faith cometh by hearing, and hearing by the word of God."

Obviously, then, it is not sufficient to merely know the Bible intellectually, or to have its records stored in the memory circuits of the mind. Many people can say perfectly the catechism of their church but are faithless in their approach both to God and to life. Knowledge often gets locked into the brain without affecting the heart, but true faith touches the heart, since faith is emotional as well as intellectual.

That the Word of God is the source of true faith is incontrovertible. It is plainly declared in the Bible, it was often illustrated by Christ as He spoke to needy ones and they responded immediately, and it is testified to by all those great heroes of faith in the eleventh chapter of Hebrews who functioned in a nearly unbelievable manner after they heard a word from God. God's Living Word—Jesus Christ, God's written Word—the Bible, and God's preached Word are all intended to produce, inspire, and direct faith, but it is not the dead letter of the written word, or the historical account of God's *Logos* (Jesus Christ), or even the rhetoric or the oratory of the preachers that produces this divine faith; it is the Living Word, which emanates from the presence of God Himself that changes our atmosphere into His atmosphere. It is God's Word on the wings of His Spirit through whatever channel He may choose that illuminates our darkness, dispels our doubts, and infuses us with His faith.

Nevertheless, man is required to be a participant in this change from natural to spiritual atmosphere, from an absence of faith to a fullness of faith. Paul declares that "hearing" is an essential condition to the reception of faith. No amount of the divine speaking of the Word will be effectual until there is a genuine hearing of that Word. First, of course, there must be an availability of the speaking, but there are few, if any, places left on our planet where God's Word is unproclaimed. Bible translations, radio and television transmissions, Christian travelers, and missionary teachers have pretty well reached all nations, although it is granted that some of us have the message in massive doses, while others seem to get it by eyedropper. But it is not how often or how much the message has been proclaimed, but in what measure it has really been heard.

Recently I left my wife home while traveling to a series of conventions as a speaker. I typed out an entire itinerary of my flight schedule and left it with her. The final entry showed that I would leave Atlanta at 11:15 P.M. and arrive in Dallas at 12:11 A.M. During the final days of the tour I discussed this with her over the phone, pointing out that I would have to rush from the conference hall right after speaking in order to catch that late plane. She assured me that she would be awaiting me, as always, but when I arrived, there was no one to meet me. Wondering what had happened, I caught a taxi home and found her soundly asleep on the bed. Before I could ask for an explanation, she

said, "Where were you? I waited for your plane for two hours
and then came home, expecting you to call me when you arrived." She had met the noon flight from Atlanta, not the
midnight flight. There had been a writing of the word, and a
speaking of the word, but not a true hearing of the word.
Probably the company in the room had distracted her from
listening carefully.

If faith is to be produced in our hearts, we must hear the
Word of God as a man listens to a will being read, or as the
accused waits to hear the sentence of the judge. What is
being said will affect us for eternity, for this is the eternal
God speaking and imparting something of the atmosphere of
His eternity into our limited sphere of "now." Careless listening will produce human frailty, not divine faith.

The provision of faith is entirely up to God, and He has
never failed in any covenant He has ever made with man.
God has not demanded faith of men and then left it up to
them to produce it; He merely asks them to receive it. God
speaks the faith into existence, requiring only that we hear it
with our hearts and speak it with our mouths. We are not the
producers of faith; we are the consumers. We do not speak
faith into existence; we speak the existing faith. What we
hear becomes what we speak, and when we say what God is
saying, marvelous things happen. But if we have been ex-
posed to faith through the hearing of the Word, and do not
respond, nothing is produced.

Adam Clarke says in volume 6 of his *Commentary*, "Preaching, God sends; if heard attentively, faith will be produced;
and if they believe the report, the arm of the Lord will be revealed in their salvation."

I have never fully understood this principle; I merely accept it. I have had people tell me that they had seen me on
television and that my teaching had inspired fresh faith in

their hearts. What they did not know was that the program they watched had been taped five years previously. I've also had people talk similarly about cassette tapes that were over ten years old, and I have sat in my study and physically wept as the presence of the Lord flowed through me while I read sermons that were written well over a hundred years ago.

God's faith is not formed in the emotions of men's minds; it is produced in His own nature and released to us through His inspired Word. Therefore we have an abundance of faith available to us at all times, and a confession of our lack of faith is probably a confession of insufficient time spent in God's presence and in His Word.

Faith cannot regenerate in man's heart, but it does tend to degenerate rather rapidly. Faith is less like the permanent magnet and far more like the electric magnet that must be energized every time it is used. Somehow our beings do not store up faith on a continuous basis; we need to be energized and reenergized by the power of the Word. Like muscular energy, faith can be exhausted and must be replenished.

God freely provides the faith; we must appropriate it. Unfortunately, we often work so hard trying to produce it that we fail to simply procure it. It is available without a price tag, without an expenditure of great energy, and without a demonstration of great righteousness. God has provided faith for every man; all he needs to do is listen to what God is saying to him through the Word.

But while faith is nonproducible and easily procurable, it is extendable—that is, when faith is present, there will also be present other Christian graces and responses that strengthen and release that faith in our normal everyday world. Since it is so difficult to think of faith without also mentioning these additives, let's look at some of the major areas into which faith can be extended.

3
Faith Extended

There is a faith that is as natural to man as the air he breathes. Witness the absolute trust and faith each newborn baby has in its mother, or the faith people evidence in machinery, public services, and government. Without this human faith, society would become a perpetual struggle for assurance. God has mercifully implanted inherent trust and faith in every human heart; it is part of the life process. But God has a divine faith that is higher, different, and far more glorious than human faith. These two faiths function in our realm of space and time, but only divine faith can function in eternity. Each faith is a gift or provision of God, and all persons have the natural faith, but only those persons who come to God through Jesus Christ will ever become partakers of this supernatural faith. This book is concerned exclusively with this faith of God that originates in Him, is transmitted by Him, and may be received and participated in by the blood-bought saints of God.

In writing about this wonderful spiritual energy the Bible calls faith, Arthur W. Pink, in his book *An Exposition of Hebrews,* declares:

> Faith shuts its eyes to all that is seen, and opens its ears to all God has said. Faith is a convictive power which overcomes carnal reasonings, carnal prejudices, and carnal excuses. It enlightens the judgment, moulds the heart, moves the will, and reforms the life. It takes us off earthly things and wordly vanities, and occupies us with spiritual

and Divine realities. It emboldens against discourage-
ments, laughs at difficulties, resists the Devil, and triumphs
over temptations. It does so because it unites the soul to
God and draws strength from Him. *Thus faith is altogether a
supernatural thing* (italics added).

Since faith is altogether a supernatural thing, there is no
way that mixing our natural faith with it can enlarge, ex-
pand, augment, extend, or increase it in any way. Jesus told
Nicodemus, "That which is born of the flesh is flesh; and
that which is born of the Spirit is spirit" (John 3:6), and
someone has added "and never the twain shall meet." We
recognize that no amount of culture, education, or affluence
can elevate natural life into eternal life. Similarly, we accept
that our natural love can never mature into divine love, for
the Scriptures clearly state, "Herein is love, not that we
loved God, but that he loved us . . ." (1 John 4:10), showing
that *agape* love flows from God to man, not the converse.
Why, then, do we so consistently speak of the enlargement of
faith as something we are capable of producing?

Faith, divine faith, is not a spiritual muscle that enlarges
with exercise; nor is it an intellect that expands by study and
speech. It is, as we shall later see, a divine gift, a spiritual
fruit, and a wholly supernatural, divine energy. It is measur-
able, for Paul declares, ". . . God hath dealt to every man the
measure of faith" (Romans 12:3), and that measure is increasable, for "the apostles said unto the Lord, Increase our
faith" (Luke 17:5), but unfeigned faith is not reproducible; it
is only receivable. Although Jesus did tell His disciples that
faith the size of a grain of mustard seed could move mountains (*see* Matthew 17:20), His emphasis was on the minute
quantity of faith required to do great exploits, not on the
living ability of a seed to grow and enlarge itself.

Only once in the entire Bible do we read of faith growing, and that is in Paul's introductory remarks in his letter to the church in Thessalonica in which he says, "We are bound to thank God . . . because that your faith groweth exceedingly . . ." (2 Thessalonians 1:3). The Greek word we have translated "groweth" is *huperauxano*, which means "to increase above ordinary degree." This is the only time in the entire Bible where it has been translated "groweth." When true growth process is signified, such as the mustard seed's phenomenal growth, the Greek word employed is *anabaino*, which means "to arise, ascend, climb, come up, or grow." If Paul had thanked God that the Thessalonian saints had successfully nurtured their faith until it had grown from a seed into a tree, he would have used *anabaino*, but deliberately he chose the word *huperauxano*, which signifies an abundant increase but does not mean that the faith had produced the increase. It was not the inherent nature of faith that caused it to increase; these saints had learned the secret of returning repeatedly to the source of faith in order to receive an ever-enlarging supply of divine energy.

"So then faith cometh by hearing, and hearing by the word of God" (Romans 10:17), not by planting a seed of faith and watching it grow. Faith is not a plant in God's garden; it is an energy inherent in His nature. We cannot plant, cultivate, nurture, or reproduce faith any more than we can raise a harvest of divine holiness, omnipotence, or mercy.

In *The Real Faith,* Dr. Charles Price, under whom it was my privilege to study in my younger days, says, "One of the chief difficulties is our failure to see that faith can be received *only* as it is imparted to the heart by God Himself. Either you have faith, or you do not. You cannot manufacture it . . . you cannot work it up. You can believe a promise, and at the same time not have the faith to appropriate it."

He later says, "No matter how much you nurture and culti-vate the spirit which the world interprets as 'faith,' it will never grow into *faith* which was introduced by Jesus in the days of long ago."

Some years ago I was associated with a church that invited a guest minister whose ministry often took him behind the Iron Curtain. His financial need was apparent, so we took up an offering to help undergird his ministry. The following week a woman in that congregation told me that God had touched her and her husband's hearts to invest money in this man's ministry. She said they had determined to give a spe-cific amount but that she had sent it instead to Mr. X (a well-known television personality). She assured me that the harvest of this seed would fully finance the guest minister's next trip to Europe.

Of course, it didn't, for faith cannot be grown, nor does giving money to one who has an obvious surplus meet the need of one who is lacking. The couple had neither obeyed God nor functioned in divine faith; they had played the well-known Christian game called "Let's Grow Faith," and left the responsibility of helping to meet this brother's finan-cial plight up to the rest of us.

In Paul's list of things the Christian should "put on," faith is conspicuous for its absence. We are challenged to put on mercies, kindness, humility, meekness, long-suffering, for-bearance, forgiveness, charity, and peace (*see* Colossians 3:12–14), but faith is not mentioned, for it can no more be "put on," in the sense of being produced or grasped, and added to life than eternal life could be "put on." Faith must be received and then lived. It is a life of faith, not an article of faith, of which the Bible speaks. It is not an addition to our lives; it is the vital energy of our lives.

Some have likened faith to the roots of a tree supporting

the main trunk and limbs, while calling the leaves and fruit the grace of God. But Dr. Charles Price denies this allegory, insisting, instead, that faith is the life force that flows into the roots and then up throughout the entire structure of the tree. For faith far more than stabilizes the Christian life, it gloriously animates it. Faith draws from the soil of the Word of God, converts it to a usable energy, and then transports it to the uttermost extremes of our life. Fortunately, it need not be understood to be experienced, for faith always works both in and through our lives to such an extent that we can be "full of faith" (Acts 6:8), "strong in faith" (Romans 4:20), and "steadfast in faith" (Colossians 2:5). We just cannot reproduce that faith.

Still, while faith is only receivable, not reproducible, it is possible to add other Christian virtues to it to round it out and give broader expression to it in our daily behavior.

Simon Peter addresses his second epistle ". . . to them that have obtained like precious faith with us . . ." (2 Peter 1:1), and says, ". . . giving all diligence, add to your faith *virtue;* and to virtue *knowledge;* And to knowledge *temperance;* and to temperance *patience;* and to patience *godliness;* And to godliness *brotherly kindness;* and to brotherly kindness *charity.* For if these things be in you, and abound, they make you that ye shall neither be barren nor unfruitful in the knowledge of our Lord Jesus Christ" (2 Peter 1:5–8, italics added).

These seven Christian graces can be added to, blended into, and harmonized with the divine faith that has been "obtained" from God, but they do not increase that measure of faith; they merely flavor it, give it texture and color, and become its fragrant aroma. They are not so much the bread crumbs in the meat loaf of faith as they are the salt, pepper, and spices.

Furthermore, none of these seven Christian excellences can ever substitute for faith, for while they are attracted to faith as steel is attracted to a magnet, they no more possess the energy of faith than nails possess the energy of a magnet. While faith may flow through all of these additions, lending its energy to and through them, they never become faith— only channels of faith.

In addition to these seven areas of goodness that should gravitate to the pure, unfeigned faith we have received from God, there are other fruits of righteousness that grow on the branches of our lives very much as individual grapes mature into a cluster. These correlate together with faith to the extent that it becomes very difficult to think of one without the other. Usually these correlatives of faith are complementary; oftentimes they are supportive, and sometimes they are expressions of God's faith in our lives.

Who can completely separate faith and love? Love is the very channel through which faith works! How can faith and hope be divided when hope is often the fountainhead out of which faith flows? Similarly, when trust is taken out of faith, or when faith seeks to operate without obedience, we have an anemic, forceless faith that may have been divine in its origins but has been greatly weakened in its operation in our lives.

As well, we find it most difficult to discuss faith without speaking of believing, or to explain faith's operation without referring to the fruit and gift of faith, for these are so integrated with our understanding of faith as to almost make them synonymous terms in our vocabularies.

But none of these realities, experiences, or actions is faith. Each is a subsidiary of faith, a portion of the parcel, a correlative of faith, but faith stands above and beyond all of them put together. Still, it seems necessary to examine the relationship of these correlatives to faith to further enhance our concept of and conduct in faith.

Perhaps we should first examine the scriptural interaction of faith and love, for no other correlative holds such a strong place in the Scriptures.

4
Faith and Love

There are some things in this life that, in spite of their dissimilarities, are almost always thought of together, as though one without the other would be incomplete. For instance, we traditionally couple bread and butter, potatoes and gravy, men and women, plus love and marriage in our minds.

Interestingly enough, God's Word couples *faith* and *love* more than a dozen times in the New Testament, for although they are different qualities, they are dependent one upon the other. Faith in Christ is the mainspring of action, and that action is regulated by the law of love; or, put another way, faith makes a man desire to do the will of God, and love tells him what that will is.

In writing to correct the error of seeking to attain righteousness by ritual observances, Paul told the Galatians, "For in Jesus Christ neither circumcision availeth any thing, nor uncircumcision; but faith which worketh by love" (Galatians 5:6). Having just declared that through the Spirit we wait "for the hope of righteousness by faith" (v. 5), Paul has again regrouped his beloved triad of faith, hope, and charity—the three abiding graces (*see* 1 Corinthians 13:13)—but, as in several other of his epistles, he has interconnected *faith* and *love* almost as closely as when he declared faith and love to be our "breastplate" (*see* 1 Thessalonians 5:8). Actually, we can separate the Christian graces only in thought, for in experience they blend and interact one with another.

The Roman Catholic idea that it is "faith made perfect by

love" actually is founded on a mistranslation, for the verb is not in the passive voice, but the middle, as always, in the New Testament. Paul is not speaking of faith being perfected; he is declaring that faith is operative: "Faith ... worketh by love." Faith is an active power. It works. It can function in the supernaturals in a most natural fashion. Faith is not merely a passive reliance upon the "finished work of Christ," or upon the grace of God, which is to do everything for us while we luxuriate in inactivity; faith—active, living faith—goes beyond an intellectual conviction of the truth and begins to operate in its own energy, discovering a field of enterprise in love. Faith shows its energy in love. Even though faith is not the highest of the virtues— love is—still we do not read of love working through faith, but of faith working through love.

As Harold Horton wrote many years ago:

> Faith touches God and brings Him to our aid in every time of need for spirit, soul, or body. Faith invades God's armory for weapons in the fight against sin, storms heaven's strong room for God's promised bestowals. Faith takes God's righteousness for man's sin—and that is salvation. Faith seizes God's fullness for man's emptiness—and that is the baptism in the Holy Spirit. Faith snatches God's health for man's sickness—which is divine healing. Faith grasps God's holiness for man's failure—which is sanctification.

While it is true that faith does grow and find its perfection in love, it is not the love that produces the faith; it is the faith that produces the love. Faith inspires love, as love reciprocally inspires faith, for when we believe in and trust the goodness of Christ we are subsequently moved to love Him.

We must first believe in His love before we can return it. Once faith has aroused love, that faith exercises itself in promoting the objects of love. We trust in the unseen God, and we also love Him; then as we try to please Him, we enjoy His favor and live in His presence. These are the goals of love, but we would never have sought these goals if we were not supported and urged on by our belief and trust in what is beyond our sight and experience.

Since faith, in the absolute sense of the word, is a personal and spiritual union with Christ through which we become one with Him as He is one with the Father, it must channel itself through love, for "God is love" (1 John 4:8). As Dr. Donald Grey Barnhouse says in his book *Romans,* "The secret of faith is a simple one—it is feeding upon Jesus Christ. This is of the utmost importance in developing our Christian life and experience." In this, faith and love must flow together proportionately. We believe His testimony of Himself intellectually, and we respond in love emotionally, all the while opening ourselves to Him spiritually.

In the story of the very sinful woman who washed the feet of Jesus with her tears and anointed His head with costly ointment, Jesus said to Simon, His host, ". . . her sins, which are many, are forgiven; for she loved much . . ." (Luke 7:47). John identifies this woman as Mary, the sister of Lazarus. In the many visits of Jesus, Mary had sat at his feet listening to Him teach of the kingdom of God. Her faith had grown exceedingly through the Word and her association with Jesus, and somehow that faith needed a release. It found its expression through the love channel as she worshipped Jesus in a most ardent manner. Her faith worked through love, and she was completely forgiven all her sins.

Paul is not telling the Galatian Christians that faith through love should do great works of beneficence, but that faith evidences its vitality and power through the love which it produces in us—faith by love operative and influential. J. B. Phillips translates this phrase as "faith which expresses itself in love." Love is viewed not as a separate action of the Spirit added on to our faith by an extrinsic effort of the soul, but as a product of that faith itself, by which faith exerts its own internal energy.

Faith expresses itself through love, so love flourishes exactly as faith flourishes. If in the midst of problems and distress, we begin to doubt the Lord's goodness and wisdom, it is not long until our hearts become cold toward God, but if in those same circumstances our faith strengthens its hold upon God and His promises, love bursts forth into full blossom. The faith and love will increase or diminish together every time.

Furthermore, though faith works by love, the love reacts upon faith and adds to its power, for love forbids unbelief. The wife who deeply loves her husband has great faith in his abilities, capacities, and character. When this trust is violated, her love begins to diminish and needs the bolstering of renewed faith. So it is in our walk in faith. Love just will not let us doubt. When the mind declares defeat and failure, love asserts its healing balm and encourages the will to hold on a little longer. Faith and love are the great allied principles of Christian life. As Dr. Perkins wrote, "Faith is the cause of love, and love is the fruit of faith."

A Puritan divine once wrote, "Faith and love are the two arms and the two eyes without which Christ can neither be seen nor embraced." We dare not play one against the other or seek to develop one more than the other. We need both of these oars if we are to row our boats to the other side. But some people mistakenly believe that one or the other virtue is sufficient. Little wonder that all of their motion results in turning circles. No amount of faith càn compensate for a lack of love, nor can an abundance of love indemnify a lack of faith.

In my book *Let Us See Jesus,* in referring to the breastplate of faith and love I write:

> For the purpose of provision, nourishment, comfort and strength, the Bride of Christ is to be well-developed, just as that of a mature woman in the natural.
>
> Some churches are very strong on faith, but they don't have much love; others have a great deal of love, but they don't have enough faith to handle the church budget. Both extremes are badly out of balance; neither has the perfect symmetry of a beautiful, fully developed woman. God wants His church to have equal development in the areas of faith and love.
>
> When it is noted that God is developing faith or love in His church, some say, "Isn't it wonderful that God is finally calling out His church?" No; He's had His church all along, but now He's emphasizing the need of full development in these areas. God allows a group to go just so far in the faith realm; then He does not allow further development until His dealings begin to produce a flow of love. Or, conversely, in the people who flow so well in love, but not so much in faith, He cuts off the love and deals in the development of faith, so there will not be a lopsided presentation of His kingdom; for God is a God of balance.
>
> When we are strong in faith and weak in love, faith does not have a proper channel to work through. This is probably why we see some very awkward things produced by men of faith who have not love. Some are always calling for "equal time" to preach their ideas, but God is calling for "equal development" for adequate presentation of His Gospel.

Faith and love are partners, but they never lose their distinct individualities. We may love Christ until we have poured out all of our spikenard upon Him and have washed His feet with our tears until we have totally exhausted the fountains of the deep within us, but this will not substitute for faith. If faith were present, this would be a channel for its release, but it cannot become the creative cause for faith any more than hope can become the causative agent for the production of love.

Faith works through love, but it is not love; nor is love a synonym for faith. Furthermore, hope, although intimately associated with both faith and love, cannot substitute for faith. Love gives faith hands and feet; hope lends it wings. Love is the fire at its heart and the lifeblood coursing in its veins, while hope is the light that gleams and dances in its eyes.

Nevertheless, we cannot ignore the fact that the Scriptures declare, "Without faith it is impossible to please him ..." (Hebrews 11:6). It is not without love, not without hope; but without *faith*. Hope is necessary and helpful, but it is not faith—but that is an additional story.

5
Faith and Hope

That Abraham was a mighty man of faith is attested to in the numerous references in the New Testament to his life of obedience. In one area of his faith, however, God seemed to sorely test Abraham. He was childless. All the benefits of his life of faith would go to the grave with him without progeny. God promised him a son, but the years passed without any visible evidence of the fulfillment of that promise. But even after Sarah went through the menopause and he himself was nearly one hundred years of age, Abraham ". . . against hope believed in hope, that he might become the father of many nations, according to that which was spoken, So shall thy seed be" (Romans 4:18). When circumstances assailed his faith, causing it to subside, hope continued to sing her lilting song, "I believe God."

As Charles Spurgeon says in *The Treasury of David,* "Hope knows her title good when she cannot read it clear. She expects the promised boon though present providence stands before her with empty hands." Abraham had a promise, but when faith seemed unable to appropriate that promise and bring it into fulfilled fact he continued to hope anyway. Hope outwaited his faith, and the interim was an opportunity to develop stronger faith, which would become "the substance of things hoped for" (Hebrews 11:1).

Hope is frequently defined as a desire accompanied by expectation, but it is not always expectant, for one may have hope with little or no expectation. A person may recognize

the possibility without embracing the probability or antici-
pating the performance. Perhaps a better definition of hope
is to call it an interest or desire whose fulfillment is
cherished, for to fulfill its true mission in the life of man,
hope needs to flow from the heart of man, not just from his
head. Hope needs to brighten the heart with expectancy in
the dark hours of fear and doubt. As Charles Spurgeon said,
"In the garden of hope grow the laurels for future victories,
the roses of coming joy, the lilies of approaching peace."
Hope gives beauty and courage to the period of life between
the promise and its performance.

It has been pointed out that animals are known to die
quickly when hopeless and to revive quickly when given new
hope. There is also medical evidence that helplessness and
hopelessness can contribute to the development of organic
disease in man. When hope vanishes, life vegetates, so Samuel Johnson was right when he observed that where there is
no hope there can be no endeavor. Three times David wrote,
"Why art thou cast down, O my soul? and why art thou dis-
quieted in me? *hope thou in God . . .*" (Psalms 42:5, 11; 43:5,
italics added). The loss of hope is the loss of strong desire and
burning expectation, which will result in despondency,
gloominess, and apathy.

While hope is not the only activating and guiding principle in man's life, it is a major factor affecting all of the
others, for none of the other factors spurs one to action without some measure of hope or certainty that his action will
satisfy or fulfill him in one way or another.

Paul listed hope as one of the three eternal graces that are
now active in men's lives. He says, "Now abideth faith, hope,
[and] charity . . ." (1 Corinthians 13:13), contrasting "abideth" to the "shall be done away" of verses 8 and 9 of this
chapter. While there are many graces of God for the believer

in this present world, only faith, hope, and love are eternal
and will endure into the next world. It may be that Paul felt
that this triad of virtues was so essentially a part of the
Christian's character that the existence of the individual
without them was unthinkable, even in eternity, for there is
no scriptural evidence that life in heaven will be static.
Heaven will afford limitless opportunities for growth, so the
finite soul will never be able to dispense entirely with faith;
and the development into the next stage of faith can be
anticipated through hope, for the sphere of hope is "things
not seen," and eternity will be full of the unseen.

Whereas the word *faith* is almost unknown in the Old Testament, *hope* flows through its pages like a sparkling brook in
a meadow. The grace of hope is peculiarly prominent in the
Old Testament, for that was the time of promise and prophecy, whereas the New Testament period is the time of fulfillment. Everything then had a forward look, for the Hebrew
golden age lay in the future; everything pointed to the coming of their Messiah. To the New Testament believer, faith is
rooted in the fulfilled promises of God even more than it is
tied to future realization. While much of the hope of Old
Testament believers was directed to temporal good, such as
health, riches, and victory in time of war, there were also
higher aspirations to their hope. The psalmists and the
prophets directed Israel's hope to the Lord, and their sacrificial principle was rooted in a hope of "better things to
come."

In the New Testament, hope has a wider range for its object and is generally more spiritual in its content, because it
is a "better hope" based on a "better covenant," which has
been enacted on "better promises." Of course, the New Testament hope also seeks blessings that are not limited to the
future life, including all that is promised to faith in this

present life. Still, the apostle Paul warns us not to focus our hope exclusively on things temporal, for he wrote, "If in this life only we have hope in Christ, we are of all men most miserable" (1 Corinthians 15:19).

It is interesting that hope is never attributed to Jesus, nor did the word ever cross His lips except for the occasion when He referred to "your hope." For Him the realities of the next world and of the future were so completely familiar that He did not need hope.

But that certainly is not the situation for today's believers in Christ. The heavenly realm is still far too unknown to us to dispense with hope. As a matter of fact, the coming of Christ and His Ascension left the church with an eschatological expectation that was primarily and almost technically the "hope" of the New Testament. Paul told Titus that ". . . we should live soberly, righteously, and godly, in this present world; Looking for that blessed hope, and the glorious appearing of the great God and our Saviour Jesus Christ" (Titus 2:12, 13). This *blessed* hope became *the* hope of the church. Its foundations were the promises of the Old Testament, the pledge given in the Resurrection of Jesus Christ, and personal devotion to Christ which gave an inner certainty to this hope, for, ". . . experience, [worketh] hope; And hope maketh not ashamed; because the love of God is shed abroad in our hearts by the Holy Ghost which is given unto us" (Romans 5:4, 5).

This passage in Romans links the operation of our faith with the production of our hope. Until faith has brought us into a peaceful relationship with God (Romans 5:1), there can be no progression from tribulation through patience, experience, and into hope (Romans 5:3, 4). The very nature of hope makes faith its inseparable condition, for hope, as a desire of future good, must be accompanied by faith to attain its realization. Faith and hope are very much like a hand and glove. Hope's animation is dependent upon faith's operation, while faith's projection lies in hope's presence.

The object both of faith and of hope is something unseen. Faith is concerned equally with past, present, or future, while *hope is directed only to the future.* Faith embraces a certainty of fulfillment; hope embraces an expectancy of desire. Faith views the promise; hope views the problem. Faith rises and falls on the crest of the waves; hope is "an anchor of the soul."

Faith and hope are complementary, but they are not interchangeable, nor, as some have suggested, are they indistinguishable one from the other. *Hope* is based on desire, facts, and rational considerations as well as, in its higher form, on faith. *Faith,* on the other hand, is based not only on facts and rational considerations, but on a sense of God's presence in one's own life, and is greatly strengthened by one's personal devotion and commitment to Christ. It is in faith that Christ Himself becomes one's hope.

Hope is a beautiful supplement to faith but a dangerous substitute for it. It can undergird faith with ceaseless joy (*see* Romans 5:2) and strengthen faith in patient doing and suffering (*see* 1 Thessalonians 1:3 and Hebrews 6:11), but it is *faith* that is "the substance of things hoped for" (Hebrews 11:1). It is faith that reaches into the unseen and grasps the object of our hope, bringing it into the reality of the life we now live in the flesh. He who substitutes hope for faith will be a perpetual dreamer. No matter how joyful or steadfast he may be in his hopes, he will never be a possessor of the things hoped for until faith begins to operate in him.

The New English Bible translates Colossians 1:4, 5 as ". . . we have heard of the faith you hold in Christ Jesus, and the love you bear towards all God's people. Both spring from the hope stored up for you in heaven—that hope of which you learned when the message of the true Gospel first came to you." In my book *Let Us See Jesus,* I comment:

> Faith and love both spring from hope. It is almost as though Paul visualized hope as a gushing fountain of pure water atop a tall mountain. Some of this water flowed down one side of the mountain, eventually forming a river of faith, while the rest of the water flowed down the opposite side of the mountain, forming a mighty stream of love, but although both streams flowed in different directions, each had its source in the same fountain. Hope is the fountainhead from which both faith and love flow. It is the quality from which faith springs and the atmosphere in which love grows. It is the Christian hope within us that fosters and ferments faith and love which flow out of us.

The issue should not be which is the greater, faith or hope, for each is complementary to the other. But if the source spring is placed for the river, all water transportation would cease, and if hope is put for faith, we may enjoy the bubbling spring of enthusiastic desire, but we will never know the life-flowing river that faith can become in the life of the believer.

If God has spoken to our hearts, our response should never be, "Well, I hope so." When God's Word is quickened to our lives, our immediate response should be, "God said it; that settles it; I believe it." Faith, not hope, is the proper response to the Word. Faith, not hope, brings forth the perfect fruit of obedience. Faith, not hope, reaches into the unseen and makes things visible. No one in the Bible asked the Lord to increase his hope, but several requested an increase in their faith.

Still, to the writer to the Hebrews, faith and hope were most integrally connected, for he wrote, "Faith is the sub-

stance of things hoped for, the evidence of things not seen"
(Hebrews 11:1). It is not the hope which looks forward with
wistful longing; it is the hope which looks forward with utter
certainty. It is not the hope which takes refuge in a perhaps;
it is the hope which is founded on a conviction. As such,
hope, when connected with faith, is only a baby step from
trust, and *trust* is the Old Testament equivalent for the New
Testament word *faith*.

6
Faith and Trust

While is is most commendable that David could cry, "[In] what time I am afraid, I will trust . . ." (Psalms 56:3), Isaiah projects a superior concept in saying, ". . . I will trust, and not be afraid . . ." (Isaiah 12:2). In commenting on this verse, Charles Spurgeon suggested that all who get aboard heaven's train will arrive in heaven, but those who join David will ride third class, while the Isaiahs will go first class.

Trust is not a product of fear; it is a preventive of fear. As a scheduled airliner tossed like a boy's kite in the storm high above the Pacific Ocean, the passengers progressed from alarm to fear, and even the stewardesses were reaching for airsickness bags. Everyone seemed to be gripped by terror—some cursed, some cried, and a few prayed—everyone, that is, except one lady traveling in the first-class section of the plane.

"How come you aren't afraid?" one passenger shouted at her.

Calmly turning her head toward the inquirer, while momentarily setting her needlepoint on her lap, she quietly said, "My husband is the pilot on this flight, and he is well qualified to get us to the airport safely."

Of course we would not have this story if they did not, in fact, arrive safely, but most of them arrived distraught, emotionally spent, and physically ill. At least one arrived calm and collected. She had trusted!

The *Merriam-Webster Dictionary* defines trust as: "(1) assured reliance on the character, strength, or truth of someone or something," and it lists confidence and dependence as synonyms.

Paraphrased with this definition, Isaiah was saying, "I will have an assured reliance on the character, strength, and truth of Almighty God, and will not be afraid."

Henry B. Smith, in his work *System of Christian Theology*, defines faith by writing, "In a general scriptural usage, faith is trusting in God's testimony—receiving all that God has revealed to us."

While *faith* is not an Old Testament word, occurring but twice in its pages, *trust* is used over 140 times in the Old Testament; whereas it appears in the New Testament less than 40 times. Even though the eleventh chapter of Hebrews credits many Old Testament characters with faith, the Old Testament speaks of their *trusting* in God. They were men and women who had a confident reliance upon God, which radically affected their attitudes and actions in life. It is not so much that they were people to be trusted, although with our hindsight we can affirm that they actually were; it is that they were people who trusted in God.

Scholars of the Old Testament Hebrew tell us that five separate Hebrew words are translated "trust." In Psalms 22:8, "He trusted on the Lord," the word *galal*, "to roll," is used. Speaking of Christ in the hours of His Crucifixion, David wrote, "He rolled himself on the Lord." What confidence and utter dependence is shown in completely rolling oneself upon the Lord. Jesus did, and it was called "trusted."

The Hebrew word *chul*, which means "to wait or stay upon," was used by Elihu when he counseled Job: ". . . therefore trust thou in him" (Job 35:14); "wait for him."

In answering his friends Job used the Hebrew word for

"hope," *yachal,* when he said, "Though he slay me, yet will I trust in him . . ." (Job 13:15). Even in the face of death Job would not relinquish his *hope,* his *trust* in God.

In at least thirty passages in the Old Testament the word *trust* comes from the Hebrew word *chasah,* which literally means "to flee for refuge." It is used when God is pictured as a rock or shield, or other protective similes. It depicts the saint seeking shelter under His wings. Psalms 91:4 affirms, "He shall cover thee with his feathers, and under his wings shalt thou trust. . . ."

By far the most frequently used Hebrew word for trust is *bathach,* which signifies "to confide in, or lean upon."

From the etymology of the Hebrew words, then, *trust* seems to be a rolling of our needs upon God, followed by a patient waiting for Him to act. It is to hope even when things seem to be hopeless and to flee to God and His promises for refuge when doubt and fear make a frontal attack upon us. To trust is to confide in God as our most trusted friend and to lean on Him as our strongest supporter.

Accordingly, both David and Isaiah are correct. Their differences lie not in their trusting, but in when they got around to trusting. David trusted after fear had gripped him, and Isaiah trusted before fear took control.

Many writers point out that everyone has trust inherent in his nature, for life in society would be impossible without it. They refer to the trust exhibited in the simple act of sitting in a chair. How long has it been since you saw someone thoroughly examine a chair before sitting down?

No, men are not without trust, for in many ways we are all trusting creatures. The redeeming or ruination that our trust will bring us hinges on the object of our trust. Who or what do we trust? Paul declares, ". . . we should not trust in ourselves, but in God . . ." (2 Corinthians 1:9), and urges Timothy to "charge them that are rich in this world, that they be not highminded, nor trust in uncertain riches, but in the living God, who giveth us richly all things to enjoy" (1 Timothy 6:17).

Dwight L. Moody is quoted as saying, "Trust in yourself, and you are doomed to disappointment; trust in your friends, and they will die and leave you; trust in money, and you may have it taken from you; trust in reputation, and some slanderous tongue may blast it; but trust in God, and you are never to be confounded in time or eternity."

"Trust in the Lord" is the repeated cry of the psalmist (for example, Psalms 37:3). "Trust ye in the Lord for ever" is the plea of the prophets (Isaiah 26:4), and "trust . . . in the living God" (1 Timothy 6:17), is the exhortation of the epistles, but what is there in God that is specifically to be depended on or trusted so implicitly that I can roll my entire life onto it?

Well, initially all of us can trust in God's self-existence, independence, and eternity. He is before all things, totally nondependent upon anything outside of Himself, and is eternally existent. He will always be around when needed.

Second, we can confide in and lean upon His veracity and infallibility, for He *is* the truth (*see* John 14:6); hence every word He speaks is the truth. "God is not a man, that he should lie" (Numbers 23:19), Balaam prophesied generations ago, and it is as factual today as it was then. Paul was willing to put the words of all men against God's Word and still believe God, for he wrote, ". . . let God be true, but every man a liar . . ." (Romans 3:4). If God said it, that settles it, for God's Word is the final rule and authority of our lives.

Third, we may confidently depend on God's omnipotence and activity. There is no limit to His ability to do. The great doxology of the Book of Ephesians cries, "Now unto him that is able to do *exceeding abundantly above* all that we ask or think,

according to the power that worketh in us, Unto him be
glory in the church by Christ Jesus throughout all ages,
world without end. Amen" (Ephesians 3:20, 21, italics
added). But God is not only able; He is active. You can
count on it! God is not a mere name; He is energetic on behalf of His people. He is the source of our life, the giver of
that life, and the sustainer of it.

Equally, we can trust most hopefully in God's expressed
love and availability. "God so loved the world, that he gave
his only begotten Son . . ." said John (John 3:16). God is not
only love by nature, but He consistently expresses that love
to us, and He makes that love unceasingly available to all of
us. We can flee to this refuge at any and all times.

David, out of personal experience, cried, "Commit thy
way unto the Lord; trust also in him; and he shall bring it to
pass" (Psalms 37:5). The Hebrew word for "commit" here is
galal, "to roll," which is often translated "trust," while the
word used for "trust" is *bathach,* "to flee for refuge." Literally,
then, he is saying, "Roll your way upon the Lord; flee to
Him for refuge; and He shall bring it to pass." God is always
trustworthy, and we have been created as trusting, dependent persons.

In speaking of trusting in God, Charles Spurgeon said,
"Trust in Christ is of the same nature in all believers. It is
not the same degree, nor in constancy, nor in energy; but it is
the same thing." I would suggest, then, that trust and faith
are not synonymous, for not only are there different degrees
in faith; there are actually different kinds of faith.

Merriam-Webster's second definition of *trust* is: "(2) a basis
of reliance, faith, or hope." Trust forms a basis for faith, but
it is not, of itself, faith.

In Robert Girdlestone's scholarly book *Synonyms and Antonyms of the Old Testament,* he declares, "Here it is to be re-

marked that though we are in the habit of speaking of faith and trust as the same thing, the Hebrew has two distinct words for them, and so has the LXX (the Septuagint, or Greek version of the Bible)."

At least some level of faith must precede trust, for a trust for the future that is not based on our present acceptance with God is a false trust and hope. It is whistling in the dark, not trusting in the Lord. All future expectation must be accompanied by a living, working faith in the present.

So while trust is an ingredient of faith, it of itself is not faith. As Paul Johanson has said, "Trust is the first fruit of faith. Without faith it is impossible to please God; without trust it is impossible for God to please us. Faith is the energy by which I take a step in God; trust is the rest by which I stand on God and His Word. Faith originates in God; my response is trust."

Faith is assurance that God will do what He says, while trust is an inner confidence that rests and waits contentedly for God's time for action. Or, as Paul Anderson teaches at Elim Bible Institute, "Trust is confidence that God will do what is best because of who He is even in the absence of a specific word."

But while trust is a commendable attitude toward faith, it is not a response action to faith. The response God is looking for is obedience without hesitation or reservation. It is a false faith if it does not invoke obedience.

7

Faith and Obedience

During the days of the Great Depression, the aged parsonage in which I was raised often vibrated with the tones of my mother's ample voice singing, "Trust and obey, for there's no other way To be happy in Jesus, But to trust and obey." Although the author of those words, Daniel B. Tower, was dead before my parents married, the truth that had been made real to him became equally real to my mother, who, with Dad, had walked away from an established business, moved hundreds of miles from their families (their first separation) to enter the ministry. They were pastoring small lumber-town churches during those years when the only work available was with the WPA, and that was unavailable to the clergy.

Mother never doubted their call to the ministry, but it frequently became an exercise of faith just to put a meal on the table for the five children. "Trust and Obey" became a theme song for Mother, for even when her faith weakened, she would trust in the goodness of God and find an inner peace that defied outer circumstances.

But Mother never did things halfway. She not only trusted; she obeyed in things great and small. She was a disciplined Bible reader and prayer warrior, and Dad rarely went anywhere to minister without Mother by his side. Again and again I watched my mother give to others out of our poverty. Mother firmly believed that if God said it, that settled it; so she obeyed it.

The men and women mentioned in the great faith chapter in Hebrews were all characterized by their implicit obedience to God. A rereading of this eleventh chapter reveals that Abel's sacrifice (v. 4) was acceptable to God because he obeyed God in bringing what God had required, while Cain's substitute was totally rejected, and that Noah (v. 7) obediently built an ark amidst the mocking of his peers, and filled that ark with provisions and animals. He obeyed God in the smallest details even while floating on the flood waters.

"By faith Abraham, when he was called to go out into a place which he should after receive for an inheritance, *obeyed;* and he went out, not knowing whither he went" (Hebrews 11:8, italics added). Abraham not only went out of Ur in obedience to God's call; he lived a life of obedience, with but a few lapses occasioned by his humanity under stress.

Furthermore, Rahab, Gedeon, Samson, David, Samuel, and others ". . . subdued kingdoms, wrought righteousness, obtained promises, stopped the mouths of lions, Quenched the violence of fire . . ." and so forth (Hebrews 11:33, 34). The writer of Hebrews merely summarizes their great exploits of faith, but the Old Testament gives us far more details of their activities, and the one predominant characteristic to be found in each of them is *obedience.* They not only believed and trusted in God's Word to them, but they obeyed it.

The word *obey* is used by the translators of the Old Testament to more fully express the verb *to hear.* It signifies the right response to "the voice" or "the word" of God. "To hear" is to be persuaded, and so to obey. David even used this form of speech when speaking of his power as an earthly king. "As soon as they hear of me, they shall obey me: the

strangers shall submit themselves unto me," he wrote
(Psalms 18:44).

It seems that to the Old Testament divines, to receive the
utterance of God in a noncommittal or merely passive fashion was virtually out of the question. They expected obedience. The only other possibility was active resistance to
God's voice, which is called *rebellion* in the Old Testament
and *disobedience* in the New Testament.

The patriarchs, prophets, and poets of the Old Testament
showed and stated that the proper and fitting response to
God's initiative is humble acquiescence which will culminate
in a combination of active obedience and unconditional
trust.

Even to the reader of the English Bible it becomes apparent that the word *obey* is used in very close association
with *believe.* The actions accompanying these two verbs are
almost indistinguishable, leaving us to feel that they could
be interchanged at will, although quite specifically the Old
Testament, perhaps because it is covenant oriented, prefers
the word *obey,* while the New Testament, which stresses the
obedience of Christ Jesus as vicarious to the believer, prefers
the word *believe.* But whether *believe* or *obey,* it is to conform in
humility to that which God prescribes by way of claim or of
promise. No other response is acceptable to God.

This close correlation between these two words is graphically illustrated in the scriptural account of the experiences
of Abraham. In writing to the church at Rome, Paul says,
"Abraham *believed* God, and it was counted unto him for
righteousness" (Romans 4:3, italics added), while in the
words attributed to God Himself we read that Abraham
"*obeyed* my voice" (Genesis 22:18; 26:5, italics added).

Repeatedly the Old Testament points out that God does

not want mere mechanical or impersonal obedience; God
desires obedience from the heart of man. He yearns for a
pattern of response that flows from a fountain of love for
God.

When my children were at home, it was a satisfying delight for me to have them obey me quickly out of a response
of love. "Sure, Daddy, right away," spoken warmly and lov-
ingly, was music equally as beautiful to me as a Brahms' lul-
laby, but when the response was grudging and obviously
against their true will, it was nearly as disappointing as disobedience.

If a man finds favor in the tail-wagging, immediate response of his favorite dog, surely God is satisfied when one of
His men or women reacts to His voice in instant, implicit,
inspired obedience. The desire to obey is equal to the deed in
the eyes of God, for the set of the soul as it hears God's voice
determines the response of the will. The person filled with
love for God will be tempered to automatically implement
what God has said, while the soul in love with itself will seek
to find a way around God's commands. It is almost the difference between a loving wife responding to her husband's
request and a corporate lawyer responding to the most recently passed congressional laws. Some Christians read the
Bible in search of those things that would please God, while
others study its pages in search of loopholes that could release them from further obligation to obey.

All who have walked with God, or have even seriously
read His Word, will agree that not all of His commands are
pleasant and agreeable. The command for Noah to build an
ark carried with it the horrible awareness of the destruction
of every living thing that was not in that ark. Abraham must
have felt an inner revulsion at God's command to sacrifice

Isaac, and Moses had many years of unpleasantness because of God's call to lead the Israelites out of Egypt. But they obeyed anyway.

God speaks not only of health, wealth, and happiness, but also of suffering, privation, and labor. We cannot pick and choose what we want to obey, for every word of God to the hearts of His children must be responded to with either a positive or a negative reaction. We either will or will not obey. There is no neutral position, nor is there ever an acceptable substitute for complete obedience, as King Saul learned when he only partially obeyed the Lord and sought to make up for it by offering a massive sacrifice unto God. ". . . To obey is better than sacrifice, and to hearken than the fat of rams," the prophet Samuel told him (1 Samuel 15:22). Because of this attempt to substitute sacrifice for obedience, God took the kingdom away from him and his progeny.

Some years ago Dr. J. R. Miller said, "It is a great deal easier to do that which God gives us to do, no matter how hard it is, than to face the responsibilities of not doing it." Obedience may be difficult at times, but disobedience is deadly at all times!

Sitting in a convention listening to one of the other team members speak, I was a little startled to hear him say, "Faith is really nothing more than obedience to God's Word," to which his audience responded with a rousing "Amen." But this is more of the simplistic theology that has brought many Christians into a feigned faith rather than a true faith. Certainly obedience is a dynamic factor in faith, but it cannot be totally equated with faith; one cannot be placed for the other.

Actually, it is possible to act in faith without acting in complete obedience to God's Word. A prophet in the Old Testament did it, for one. Told to go from Judah to Bethel to prophesy against Jeroboam's altar to the golden calves and to return home by a different route without stopping for food or water, this man of God went, prophesied, withstood King Jeroboam with mighty signs and wonders, and then started home as commanded. But an older prophet pursued him, claiming that God had given an additional message instructing the man of God to turn aside, eat, and rest. When he finally resumed his journey, a lion slew him, but not his donkey, and the two animals stood side by side by the slain prophet until someone took the body for burial. "And when the prophet that brought him back from the way heard thereof, he said, It is the man of God, who was disobedient unto the word of the Lord: therefore the Lord hath delivered him unto the lion, which hath torn him, and slain him, according to the word of the Lord, which he spake unto him" (1 Kings 13:26).

Furthermore, it should be possible to function in complete obedience without flowing in faith. Fear motivation drove the Israelites to obey their taskmasters in Egypt, and later in the wilderness the lack of an alternative caused them to obey God in following the cloud through the wilderness. The divine provision of food, water, protection, and guidance prevailed only where the cloud rested. Obedience was based on necessity, but God did not credit this as faith.

The brokenhearted cry of God's heart throughout the entire Old Testament was over the disobedience of His people. It seemed that no matter how He blessed them, communicated with them, and provided for them, they took what they wanted and did as they pleased. They were selfish and self-centered, stubborn and sinful. It almost seems that they would rather climb a tree and be disobedient than stand on the ground and obey.

How the prophets cried on God's behalf, ". . . Obey my

voice, and I will be your God, and ye shall be my people: and walk ye in all the ways that I have commanded you, that it may be well unto you" (Jeremiah 7:23). Some did; many did not.

How little the Church has learned from history. We continue to ignore the multiple lessons of the Old Testament and still try to exercise miracle faith without first bringing our lives into obedience to God's voice and Word. Why do we so earnestly expect the fulfillment of a prophetic utterance in a conference or church service without also obeying the condition stated in the *rhema* word as reinforced by the written *logos?* Remember that after the prophet Zechariah had given a glowing prophecy of the coming of Christ to the Jews and of the reestablishing of His kingdom among them, he qualified it by saying, ". . . And this shall come to pass, if ye will diligently obey the voice of the Lord your God" (Zechariah 6:15). This, of course, does not make the obedience the cause of the fulfillment of the prophecy, but it does become a condition for its fulfillment, for most of God's written promises are conditional: "I will if you will."

Obedience is a necessary response to faith, and great faith demands complete obedience, both of Old Testament and New Testament saints. The only difference is that the New Testament not only demands obedience, but also requires an act of believing from those who would make faith work for them; but that is still another situation.

8
Faith and Believing

What *obedience* is in the Old Testament, *believing* becomes in the New Testament; it is the divinely accepted response to the quickened Word of God when God communicates with an individual.

When God speaks, something always happens. All of creation was spoken into existence by God. "God said, Let there be . . . and there was . . ." (Genesis 1:3). Throughout the Old Testament, God's voice, even when spoken through a human representative, was powerful enough to part the Red Sea, open the earth, close the heavens, stop the sun, and bring forth a river out of a rock. Similarly, as Jesus walked on our tiny planet, all creation instantly responded to His voice: Water, plants, fish, animals, and weather all obeyed Him gladly.

Nothing can remain the same after God speaks to it, "For the word of God is quick, and powerful, and sharper than any twoedged sword, piercing even to the dividing asunder of soul and spirit, and of the joints and marrow, and is a discerner of the thoughts and intents of the heart" (Hebrews 4:12). Since God's Word has the power to pierce, divide, and discern in the life of people, this action will precipitate a reaction, for the energy of God's Word is a cause that demands an effect. In the New Testament that reaction, or effect, is called *believing*.

The fundamental distinction between *faith* and *believe* is not always obvious. Even the *Funk and Wagnalls New Practical Dictionary of the English Language* defines faith as "1. A firm belief in what another states, affirms, or testifies, simply on the ground of his truth or veracity," thereby using the verb *believe* to define the noun *faith;* but a noun describes a person, place, or thing, while a verb gives action to that defined person, place, or thing. It does not stand or substitute for the noun; the verb gives motion to it. Hence *believe* cannot always, and probably should very seldom, stand for *faith.*

Because the same Greek word forms the root for *faith* and *believe,* these two words are so integrally connected that it is difficult to think of them separately, but it is desirable to do so since the New Testament seems to make a consistent distinction between them by the context that surrounds them. Having already stated that a Word from God, a *rhema,* is an action originating in God Himself, while our response to that action is a reaction of believing or doubting, it follows, then, that faith has its source in God, while believing has its origins in persons. Faith, as a divine commitment, requires believing as a human confession of God's committal.

Faith is a force received; believing is that force released. Jesus told His disciples, ". . . If ye have faith as a grain of mustard seed, ye shall say unto this mountain, Remove hence to yonder place; and it shall remove; and nothing shall be impossible unto you" (Matthew 17:20). Here faith is the force, while the believing is evidenced in the saying. Faith was a conviction, while believing was a confession of that conviction.

Perhaps it would be fair to say that faith is God's attitude shared with man, while believing is man's action based on that attitude. Faith is an assurance, and believing is our assent to it. Faith is an affirmation; belief is an admission. Faith is the confidence; believing is the credence. Faith is trust; believing is obedience. Faith is a God-given ordinance; believing is our observance of that ordinance.

If faith is a reliance, then believing would be a response. If faith is a persuasion, then believing must be the performance. If faith is a cause, then surely believing would be its effect.

Robert Girdlestone, again in his book *Synonyms and Antonyms of the Old Testament,* states, "The man who believes God is he who, having received a revelation from Him, realizes it, and acts upon it as true." Any such revelation produces faith, for "faith cometh by hearing, and hearing by the word of God" (Romans 10:17), and that faith inspires believing, as on the day of Pentecost when ". . . many of them which heard the word believed; and the number of the men was about five thousand" (Acts 4:4).

It would be doctrinally and practically accurate to say that faith is the *eye* of the soul, which looks out toward God's promises and represents them clearly and convincingly to us, while believing is the *hand* of the soul, which lays hold of the contents of those promises and applies them to human behavior. Arthur W. Pink, in *An Exposition of Hebrews,* says, ". . . when the Holy Spirit renews the heart, the prevailing power of unbelief is broken; faith argues 'God has said it, so it *must* be true.' Faith so convinces the understanding that it is compelled, by force of arguments unanswerable, to believe the certainty of all God has spoken. The conviction is so powerful that the heart is influenced thereby, and the will moved to conform thereto." Pink is accurate in saying that "faith so convinces the understanding that it is compelled . . . to believe," for every action has a reaction. Faith's purpose is to produce performance; faith expects to be coupled with believing, and it is fruitless until it is so united.

The *Ellicott New Testament Commentary* reminds us that

". . . every genuine act of faith is the act of the whole man, not of his understanding alone, not of his affection alone, not of his will alone, but of all three in their central, aboriginal unity. And thus faith becomes the faculty in man through which the spiritual world exercises its sway over him, and thereby enables him to overcome the world of sin and death."

To suggest, then, that faith is an act of the head, while believing is an act of the heart, or its converse, as stated by Joseph Force Newton, "Belief is a truth held in the mind; faith is a fire in the heart," is overly simplistic in its theology, for unfeigned faith must be an act of the entire person, spirit, soul, and body. We hear and then we heed; we see and subsequently respond, and our inner knowing is translated to an outer act of believing. Believing is the only acceptable response to faith that is taught in the New Testament.

After the death and Resurrection of Jesus, Thomas, one of His disciples, openly refused to believe the testimony of the remaining ten disciples to Christ's Resurrection. Eight days later Jesus appeared to all eleven disciples at one time and said, "Thomas, Reach hither thy finger, and behold my hands; and reach hither thy hand, and thrust it into my side: and be not faithless, but believing" (John 20:27). The process used to bring Thomas from faithlessness to faith was not merely a change in his mental attitude, but involved the physical activity of seeing and touching. The faith Christ's presence produced was released in believing action; one supported the other, but it was not until action released his faith that Thomas was turned from "doubting Thomas" into "believing Thomas."

So it is with us. Truth, no matter how reinforced it may be, does not vitally affect our lives until we act on that truth in a believing demonstration of obedience, joyful response of praise, or active participation in the promise, for believing gives action to our faith.

There is a theological position that takes an almost opposite position from the one I have projected. That view suggests that *belief* may be a very impersonal, intellectual process as the acceptance of something as true on grounds other than personal observation and experience, and that as soon as this belief is strong enough to be followed by a definite action, the belief becomes faith. While this may define natural faith and believing, it cannot be accepted as descriptive of divine faith and believing, for this puts the source of faith in man's actions, while the Scriptures declare that God is the source of our faith. No matter how strong intellectual assent may become, it cannot produce or metamorphose into faith any more than an intensification of feeling can produce fact. Faith is always the cause; believing is the effect. Increasing the effect cannot produce the cause, for the formula, "To every action there will be an equal reaction," demands an increase of action to gain an increase of reaction. An increase of faith should produce an increase of believing, but extending the believing while calling it faith is feigned, not unfeigned, faith.

Since faith has its source in God and is channeled through the communication of His Word, it is the developing of a more intimate relationship with God that increases one's measure of faith, not the enlarging of one's intellectual concepts or emotional responses.

This is not to minimize the place of believing, for it is our believing that releases faith and brings us into obedience to what God has said. James Hastings has pointed out that *faith* and *believe* occur about 240 times each in the New Testament. However, if *Strong's Concordance* is consulted, it is easy to see that various forms of the word *believe* actually appear

over 400 times in the Bible, with most of them being in the
New Testament. Of course, not all are references to believing
God. Nonetheless, the Bible unquestionably speaks more of
man's believing than it does of God's faith.

This does not make *believing* more valuable than *faith;* it is
mentioned more frequently because it is a response of the individual and as such needs far more instruction, injunction,
and inspiration. Since it is something God cannot do for us,
He must then work carefully with us, for His faith is impotent in our lives until we respond in believing. John's closing
comment in his Gospel says, "But these [things] are written,
that ye might believe that Jesus is the Christ, the Son of God;
and that believing ye might have life through His name"
(John 20:31). Some of God's Word produces faith; much of it
channels that faith into believing, so that we can experience
and enjoy the life that flows from God in His *rhema* to the believer.

Faith and believing are as inseparable as incense and fra-
grance. They are coupled together like love and marriage or
clouds and rain. It is the first (faith) that induces the second
(believing), and when they are properly blended they produce a third quotient; something results. Incense and fra-
grance produce an emotional sensation; love and marriage
effect a family; clouds and rain yield productivity on the
earth; and faith and believing will bring spiritual realities
into our natural world. But for all of their dependence one
upon the other, faith and believing are not synonymous.

In the first volume of his four-volume *Dictionary of the Bible,*
Dr. James Hastings, in writing on the subjective nature of
faith, says:

> It consists neither in assent or in obedience, but in a re-
> liant trust in the invisible Author of all good (Hebrews

11:27), in which the mind is set upon the things that are above and not on the things that are upon the earth (Colossians 3:2). The examples cited in Hebrews eleven are themselves enough to show that the faith there commended is not a mere belief in God's existence and justice and goodness, or crediting of His word and promises, but a practical counting of Him faithful (Hebrews 11:11), with a trust so profound that no trial can shake it (Hebrews 11:35), and so absolute that it survives the loss of even its own pledge (Hebrews 11:17).

So unfeigned faith is not mere obedience, mental assent, or sincere belief. These may and should shape, form, and release faith, but faith that is not hypocritical will be a giant step above all of these. Actually, unfeigned faith, as taught in the New Testament, will even stand head and shoulders above THE Faith into which we so often flee for refuge when faced with disturbing doubts.

9

Faith and *the* Faith

In years gone by in his conferences both in England and America, Harold Horton used to declare:

> Faith is difficult only in its absolute simplicity. Faith is not grasping tight and clenching fists and furrowing brows and gritting teeth and shouting in a kind of hopeless hope, "I will believe; I do believe." No; that is not faith. Faith is the easy, restful, fearless attitude of an infant reposing on its mother's breast—with no thought of fear, effort, or uncertainty. Faith is absolute rest in God, absolutely knowing and absolutely trusting according to His gracious promises and commands.

The simplicity of faith has become a stumbling block to our complex society that has become accustomed to the computer, color television, and space exploration. Since we have so few simple things left in our lives, we tend to catalog faith along with a walk down a country lane, or homemade ice cream. We generally see faith as something in our pasts that has been superseded by an improved product. It is factual, as Matthew Henry puts it, that "True faith is an old grace, and has the best plea to antiquity: it is not a new invention, a modern fancy. The eldest and best men that ever were in the world were believers. They were an honour to their faith, and their faith was an honour to them. It put them upon doing the things that were of good report." But it is not truthful to say that faith has been superseded by an improved product in our generation. While faith in God has steadily been replaced by faith in science and faith in humanity, only the blind and biased would call it an improvement. Let the record speak for itself. Compare our society of fifty years ago with its present condition and see what replacing faith in God with humanism has done to us.

It is the will of God that we grow in our faith (*see* 2 Thessalonians 1:3), not grow out of our faith. It is progression, not replacement, that God desires.

The Old Testament is a prime example of this principle. The entire patriarchal story is presented to exhibit the lives of the servants of God as lives of faith, and it was their implicit self-commitment to God that set them apart as different from other men. The patriarchal religion was essentially a religion of promise, and their response was that of trust. Their walk was described as a walk "with God" and consisted in the ordering of their lives by entire trust in God, and it expressed itself in their conduct growing out of this trust. The righteousness of the patriarchal age was simply a manifestation in life of an entire surrender to God and His will in unwavering trust in His promise. This, the Book of Hebrews declares, was a life of faith.

The life of faith was not only profitable but prolific; the few partriarchs enlarged into families, and then into a full nation of people who were challenged to embrace the promises made to their fathers and to perpetuate the life of faith that had been exemplified before them. As this nation was being led by Moses toward the Promised Land, God Himself spoke to them, later writing down what He had said in the law and the commandments. As Dr. Hastings has observed, "The law-giving was not a setting aside of the religion of promise, but an incident in its history; and the law given was not a code of jurisprudence for the world's government, but a body of household ordinances for the regulation of God's family. It is therefore itself grounded upon the promise; and it grounds the whole religious life of Israel in the grace of the covenant God."

The purpose of the law was not to be a replacement for faith but to be a repository of faith and a regulation of that faith. It codified the promises and directed Israel to proper responses of faith. Inasmuch as the ultimate promise of the law and the prophets was that of a coming Messiah, the law gave direction to their lives until the Messiah came, for, as Paul points out, "The law was our schoolmaster to bring us unto Christ, that we might be justified by faith" (Galatians 3:24). The communication of promise to the patriarchs was faith in the active sense, while the codified promises in the law were a passive form of faith.

In the New Testament this passive form of faith is generally preceded by the definite article—*the* faith. Following the early events in the brand-new church, the Book of Acts records, "And the word of God increased; and the number of the disciples multiplied in Jerusalem greatly; and a great company of the priests were obedient to the faith" (Acts 6:7). Already the experience of the Day of Pentecost with the subsequent teaching of the apostles had been sufficiently codified to be called *the* faith, and a "great company of the priests" were willing to step out of the old system into the new.

Paul was unknown to the churches of Judaea, "But they had heard only, That he which persecuted us in times past now preacheth the faith which once he destroyed" (Galatians 1:23). This report was sufficient for them to open their arms to welcome Paul as a beloved brother. They felt safe in knowing that Paul had embraced *the* faith.

When Paul returned again to Lystra, Iconium, and Antioch to encourage the converts, he went ". . . exhorting them to continue in *the* faith, and that we must through much tribulation enter into the kingdom of God" (Acts 14:22, italics added).

The faith in the New Testament is the systematic declaration of the promises of God; it is the doctrines that grow out of the embraced promises given to us by God. It is a set of propositions, or a religious creed, or an article of belief that germinates out of an intimate association with God and His Word. It is no more a replacement of faith than the law was a replacement of promise. It becomes a foundation, a support, an undergirding for our faith. It is a guide, a compass, and a checkpoint for our faith. It is our safety in hearing from God, for every communication of a *rhema* is subject to what has already been declared in the *logos*.

The development of *the* faith, as we now know it, was progressive and involved a plurality of authors. Inasmuch as the Old Testament revelation of God was always incomplete, the eyes of the saints were consistently directed to the future. While waiting for the salvation of Israel, the saint was urged to stay himself on God, fixing his heart on Jehovah as the Rock and strength and trust of His people. But when Jesus came, the Gospel writers reveal that all that Jesus did and taught was directed to drawing faith to Himself. It was no longer future, but ". . . the kingdom of heaven is at hand" (Matthew 3:2). Everywhere Jesus offered Himself as the object of faith, and claimed faith in Himself to be the highest concern of the soul. In all of His dealings with His followers, His primary care was to build up their faith in Him, even in His last agonizing hours on this earth.

The Book of Acts shows how the faith of these apostles in whom Jesus had built faith persuaded many to come into obedience to the faith that is in Jesus, and they quickly gathered together a community of "believers" (*see* Acts 2:44; 4:4, 32) who brought into the infant church many old tendencies of thinking. The task of instructing and disciplining the new community soon became unavoidably one of the heaviest of apostolic duties; and its progress is naturally reflected in their letters.

To Paul fell the serious task of teaching the fundamental principle of the gospel of grace, that the righteous shall live by faith, in contrast to the ingrained legalism of Jewish thought that had intruded into the Christian Church. He taught that it is because faith lays hold of Jesus Christ that there is no room for any righteousness of our own as the grounds of our salvation.

In the Epistle to the Hebrews it is the general idea of faith, or the subjective nature of faith, that is dwelt upon rather than its specific object. These readers were not threatened with legalism, as were Paul's, but with "shrinking back" (*see* Hebrews 10:32), and so the author needed to emphasize the duty of faith far more than the object of faith, as Paul emphasized.

To James fell the responsibility of rebuking the Jewish tendency to conceive of the faith that was pleasing to God as a mere intellectual acquiescence to His being and claims. Peter spoke of faith as a power to assist in the completion rather than the inception of salvation, for he was writing to a persecuted segment of the church and sought to quicken in his readers a new hope that would sustain them in their persecutions, and to get their eyes off their trials and onto faith's very nature and the unseen and eternal glory.

John, on the other hand, wished to lay stress on the very opposite aspect of faith. John's treatment of faith is insistence not so much on the certainty and glory of the future inheritance that it secures as on the fullness of the present enjoyment of salvation that it brings, for John was writing to a church that was suffering with a false emphasis on knowledge, which tended to despise simple faith. They needed to see faith operating in the nasty here and now, not merely in the beautiful by and by.

None of the writers who were used of the Holy Spirit to define, describe, or delineate faith intended to replace subjective faith with objective faith. Rather, they were like Jude, who wrote, "Beloved, when I gave all diligence to write unto you of the common salvation, it was needful for me to write unto you, and exhort you that ye should earnestly contend for the faith which was once delivered unto the saints" (Jude 3), or the Apostle Paul who urged the saints at Philippi to ". . . stand fast in one spirit, with one mind striving together for the faith of the gospel" (Philippians 1:27).

Since our concept of God will greatly affect the level and attitude of our faith, it is important that we regularly read, seriously study, and constantly contemplate the doctrines of God's Word, for none of us will live long enough to learn the full life of faith on a trial and error basis, but ". . . these things happened unto them for ensamples: and they are written for our admonition, upon whom the ends of the world are come" (1 Corinthians 10:11). The successes and failures of the life of faith are faithfully recorded in the Scriptures as object lessons for those who yearn to learn to live by faith. The instruction and teaching on faith as shared by the New Testament writers is to enable others to embrace the principles of faith in Jesus Christ and the subsequent blessings and benefits a life of faith can bring to the believing saint.

But these examples and instructions that form *the* faith dare not become a substitute for or a replacement of God's faith, which is imparted into the heart of the believer by His divine *rhema*. The fact that the Bible records a truth or a promise does not make it a quickened Word of God to our individual lives. This requires a specific work of the Holy Spirit in the believer. Whenever we mistake *the* faith for God's faith we are doomed to failure and subsequent confusion in trying to exercise that faith. *The* faith is passive; God's faith is active. *The* faith defines, while God's faith does. *The* faith affects attitude; God's faith begets action. Each needs the other, but neither can substitute for the other. We cannot live without the teaching of the Word, but we also cannot function without the flow of divine faith. We need both the passive and the active aspects of faith in our lives, and we need to know the difference between the two. Peter would never have succeeded in walking on the water if he had tried to function on a written promise from the prophets, but he had a living word from Christ Jesus Himself. He had a *rhema*, an active word of faith. So must we!

Ideally, then, we will be both Bible students and intimate friends with Christ, for the highest level of faith flows out of an in-depth relationship with Jesus Christ. Faith, as we shall see, flows out of fellowship with God.

10
Faith and Fellowship

Few serious Christians have any difficulty with John's clear declaration that ". . . God is love; and he that dwelleth in love dwelleth in God, and God in him" (1 John 4:16), or his companion statement, ". . . God is light . . . if we walk in the light, as he is in the light, we have fellowship one with another . . ." (1 John 1:5, 7). We do not expect to receive divine love and light apart from the divine presence, for they are not imparted separate from God but are shared as we fellowship with Him. "The Lord is my light . . ." the psalmist declared (Psalms 27:1), and John affirms, "Herein is love, not that we loved God, but that he loved us . . ." (1 John 4:10). God and His nature are obviously inseparable; to share His nature we must fellowship His person.

Why, then, do we so conscientiously try to obtain ". . . the faith of the Son of God . . ." (Galatians 2:20) apart from the presence of the Son of God? If, indeed, Jesus is the ". . . author and finisher of our faith . . ." (Hebrews 12:2), then it is both vain and hypocritical to try to have faith independent from His presence. Unfeigned faith never seeks any source other than God.

In Dr. Luke's account of the storm on the Sea of Galilee, he says that after the sleeping Jesus was awakened and fearfully told of their danger, ". . . Then he arose, and rebuked the wind and the raging of the water: and they ceased, and there was a calm. And he said unto them, *Where is your faith?*"

(Luke 8:24, 25, italics added). Dr. Charles Price comments on this in his great book *The Real Faith* by saying:

> Their *Faith* was with them all the time. The mistake they made was in forgetting the *fact* of His *presence,* while discerning the *fact* of the storm . . . .
>
> Roll on, blue waves of Galilee! Blow and moan, ye winds that rage, and ye tempests that blow. You laugh at my seeming helplessness. You ridicule my endeavors to stand in the midst of the rocking of the boat. You ask me where my faith is. You taunt me about my condition. My Faith is not far away! He sleeps awhile, to teach me to rely upon Him. He sleeps, that confidence in self might be turned to trust in His promise and in the power of His presence. No, my Faith is not far away. I look at Him and smile; for His voice whispers to this poor heart of mine, and tells me that if He can rest in the midst of the tempest and storm, then I can sweetly rest in Him.

When we recognize that our faith is ultimately in Jesus, not in ourselves, we will cease introspective searchings for our faith when a crisis comes, and we will rest silently in the security of the presence of Jesus. Like the child whose fear of the dark disappears the moment Daddy sits on the edge of the bed, so the awareness of His person enables us to transfer our anxieties and fears to His loving care. He is our faith; He is perfect faith. Intimate fellowship with Him is our best assurance of continuing faith.

Jesus warned His disciples, ". . . without me ye can do nothing" (John 15:5). The Greek word we have translated here as "without" is *chōris,* which signifies "at a space—separately." "Apart from me you can do nothing at all" (PHILLIPS) is a much better translation, especially when we realize the context is speaking of the union of the branch to the vine. Yet in spite of this clear warning from the lips of Jesus, Christians still try to function apart from a vital union with Christ, declaring that they have "faith." They may, indeed, have an earthly or natural faith, such as is evidenced in depositing money in a bank, and they may have a measure of belief in scriptural principles, but they cannot have dynamic, divine faith without the presence of the Son of God, who authors and completes true faith.

Both Bible and secular history reveal that men of great faith have also been men of intimate relationship with the Lord. In the preceding chapter I stated that "The entire patriarchal story is presented to exhibit the lives of the servants of God as lives of faith, and it was their implicit self-commitment to God that set them apart as different from other men." But we have to come to the New Testament to find their lives called lives of faith. In the Old Testament it was called walking with God.

Enoch, according to Hebrews 11, walked with God and God translated him. Abraham walked with God out of Ur into Canaan, and his son Isaac, and subsequently his grandson Jacob, also walked with God. The secret of their faith was the intimate relationship they had developed with God. They talked with Him, reasoned with Him, covenanted with Him, and dared to obey Him. Their faith was not a self-energizing force; it was a by-product of a living alliance with the God of all faith.

Daniel did not go into the lions' den with lion-controlling faith, but he did enter their lair with the presence of God, just as Shadrach, Meschack, and Abed-nego did not possess fire-walking faith but were preserved by the presence of the Son of God. None of the four declared they would be deliv-

ered—only that God was able to deliver them. It was the
faith of God they shared by relating with Him over the years
that gave them deliverance in their dark hour. Without Him
(apart from Him) they would have perished.

So then faith requires more than a desperate situation, a
demanding need, or a dependable promise. Faith flows out
of a living, loving correlation between the saint and the Savior. The union of Christ with the individual believer becomes the absolute of faith.

Samson is at once the most classic and clear example of
faith flowing out of personal relationship with God. When
the Spirit of the Lord came upon Samson he was able to do
physical feats unheard of before his time—from slaying a
thousand well-equipped Philistine soldiers, using nothing
but the jawbone of a defunct donkey, to the carrying away of
the doors of the gate of the Philistine city of Gaza, all the
way to the top of the hill in front of Israel's city of Hebron,
some thirty miles away.

The secret of Samson's great strength was not in his skele-
tal or muscular structure but in the coming of God's Spirit
upon him. Scholars tell us that the phrase, "The Spirit of the
Lord came upon him," (Judges 14:19; 15:14), could accu-
rately be translated, "The Lord clothed Himself with
Samson." That is intimate and dynamic affinity. It was an
Old Testament foretaste of the New Testament reality of
". . . Christ in you, the hope of glory" (Colossians 1:27).

This is underscored by the fact that when he finally told
Delilah the key to his consecration to God, and she had a
barber shave his head, Samson arose to meet his attackers
unsuccessfully for ". . . he wist not that the Lord was departed from him" (Judges 16:20). No Spirit—no strength.

"Separated from me ye can do nothing at all."

The Schaff-Herzog Encyclopedia quotes Schoberlein as saying:

The object of faith cannot be seen with the eyes, nor can it be grasped by the understanding; it belongs to the realm of the invisible, the spiritual, the divine. But this invisible, spiritual, divine, is not something unknowable; it proves itself to the inner man. *The absolute object of faith is the revelation of God to mankind,* originating in his love, and making his holiness manifest; and the centre of this revelation ... is the incarnation of God in Christ Jesus. *Faith,* in the absolute sense of the word, *is,* therefore, *a personal union with Christ,* through which we become one with him, as he is one with the father (italics added).

Faith, therefore, cannot be apart from Christ since it actually is a part of Christ. The more vital our union with Him is, the more vital His faith will be in us. To share His nature we must share His presence; we must learn to fellowship with Christ.

Both Paul and John speak of this fellowship. Paul wrote, "God is faithful, by whom ye were called unto the fellowship of his Son Jesus Christ our Lord" (1 Corinthians 1:9), while John exclaimed, ". . . and truly our fellowship is with the Father, and with his Son Jesus Christ" (1 John 1:3). Each writer uses the same Greek word for "fellowship"— *koinōnia*—which signifies "participation or partnership." It is far stronger than our English word *fellowship,* which often means little more than social conversation. Our fellowship with Christ, in the New Testament sense, is a partnership with Him, an active association with Him, a patent participation with Him both in things touching our world and His realm.

Oswald Chambers, in his great devotional book *My Utmost for His Highest,* also expresses my premise that unfeigned faith is inseparable from fellowship with God. He says,

"Faith is the whole man rightly related to God by the power of the Spirit of Jesus Christ." Earlier in his book, he had written, "Faith is not a pathetic sentiment, but robust vigorous confidence built on the fact that God is holy love. You cannot see Him just now, you cannot understand what He is doing but you know *Him*. . . . Faith is the heroic effort of your life; you fling yourself in reckless confidence on God."

In speaking further of faith, Mr. Chambers also wrote, "Faith is not intelligent understanding; faith is deliberate commitment to a Person, where I see no way. . . . Faith never knows where it is being led, but it loves and knows the One Who is leading. . . . The root of faith is the knowledge of a Person."

That Person to whom faith makes commitment and in whom it finds its roots is our Lord Jesus Christ, for He, and He only, is ". . . the author and finisher of [*our*] faith" (Hebrews 12:2). I bracketed the italicized word *our* because it has been supplied by the translators, but it is not in the Greek manuscript. Jesus begins and completes faith; it starts with Him and ends in Him. Faith apart from Him cannot be divine faith, and no other form of faith will move God on our behalf.

In *The Real Faith* Dr. Price says, "It is not by imitation but by *participation* that we become LIKE NATURE—LIKE SUBSTANCE, 'because as He is, so are we in this world' (1 John 4:17)." Therefore, merely saying what He said, or even believing what He believed, is not unfeigned faith. We must become what He was; we must share His intimate fellowship with the Father; we must be partakers of His divine nature if we would experience the forceful flow of genuine faith.

This need of being a participant in the divine nature in order to be a channel of divine faith is realizable, for the Holy Spirit assures us, "Whereby are given unto us exceeding great and precious promises: that by these ye might be partakers of the divine nature, having escaped the corruption that is in the world through lust" (2 Peter 1:4). By action of the Spirit through the promises of the Word we become participants in the divine nature and enjoy a flow of unfeigned faith. It merely requires a submitting of ourselves to Him and His Word. Some have reduced this theme to the simple acrostic:

F–orsaking

A–ll

I

T–rust

H–im

When we can say "mission accomplished" to this, we will see faith as a principle, a power, a fruit, and a gift of the Spirit operating in and through our lives. The fruit of faith particularly works *in* us, while the gift of faith works *through* us, as we will see in the next two chapters.

11

Faith and Fruit

That faith, as a fruit, is indeed a force that is working *in* us is taught by Paul when he contrasts the horrendous works of the flesh with the harmonious fruit of the Spirit. He writes, "But the fruit of the Spirit is love, joy, peace, longsuffering, gentleness, goodness, *faith,* meekness, temperance: against such there is no law" (Galatians 5:22, 23, italics added).

I am fully aware that at least half of the modern-language translations of the New Testament substitute the word "faithfulness" or "fidelity" for the word "faith," but I am at a complete loss to understand why. The Greek word Paul used here in Galatians is *pistis,* which is exactly the same Greek word he uses for "faith" in all of his epistles. Elsewhere in the New Testament where the word "faithfulness" is used, it comes from the Greek word *pistos,* which is, of course, a form of *pistis* but is not a true substitute for it. *Pistis* fundamentally means "persuasion; credence," while *pistos* means "trustworthy; faithful." I would not pretend to have the expertise in Koiné Greek that the translators have, but I have an inner suspicion that they may have let their doctrinal concepts shade their fidelity to the language. Being "faithful" cannot be synonymous with having "faith," for faith is a divine energy while faithfulness and fidelity are actions or responses. In the *Pulpit Commentary* we read:

> It is curious to find faith seventh, and not first in this list
> of graces. Faith is the root-principle of all graces. It goes

before love itself, for it "worketh by love," and it precedes joy and peace, which both spring from our believing (Romans xv. 13). It has, therefore, been suggested that faith is here taken for fidelity. There is no reason, however, for any departure from its usual meaning. Faith is here regarded not as the means of salvation or as the instrument of our justification, but as the principle of Christian life, which controls and guides it. Thus faith supplies the strength of self-control, that is implied in temperance, and is the secret spring of that meekness which is an ornament of great price.

This limited work is not the place for an expanded apology on whether it should be "faith" or "faithfulness." Allow me to be comfortable in my awareness that the Holy Spirit, who does all things well, chose to use the word *pistis* when listing the fruit of the Spirit, and in doing so He reveals to us that there is an inner working, a progressive dealing of Himself within our lives, that contributes to the operation of divine faith. Faith is not only a force without us; it is a fruit within us. It is not only obtainable by the Christian; it is observable by his friends. Faith is, indeed, an acquired grace, but it becomes an adorning grace as well, and while it is a strength to the possessor, it is a stimulant to the observer that often creates in him an appetite for that fruit.

There are two or three rather obvious truths that are generally pointed out when the fruit of the Spirit is being discussed. The first is that although Paul speaks of the works (plural) of the flesh, he clearly speaks of the fruit (singular) of the Spirit. It is not an assortment of fruit such as one may find in a family orchard or in a fruit salad, but a single fruit with multiple appendages, as a stalk of bananas or a cluster of grapes. It is as though Paul gives individual grapes a separate name, but each grape, although it is an entity in its own right, grows on one central stem, forming a united cluster of fruit. Similarly, the manifestation of the Spirit in our lives may be varied, but it is all one fruit. It is not divided up throughout the Church, as the gifts of the Spirit often are, but each individual through whom the Spirit is producing fruit will have a demonstration of all these nine individual "grapes." The Spirit does not choose one person to be a demonstration of love, another to manifest peace, and a third to mature into joy; He desires that each Christian in whom He dwells will allow a full cluster to grow and mature in his life.

A second almost self-evident fact about the fruit of the Spirit is that the portrayal logically divides itself into three groups of three descriptions. The first three—love, joy, peace—seem logically to develop toward God and are the first to ripen in the believer. The second triad—long-suffering, gentleness, goodness—seem to develop in our relationship with our fellow man, while the third trio—faith, meekness, temperance—comprises fruit that ripen in the believer's relationship to himself and are usually the very last to come into sweetness and full maturity. The Holy Spirit causes us to become fruitful in our relationships with God, with others, and with ourselves. He makes us to be a fragrant aroma, a stimulating sight, and a satisfying flavor to Him Who is above us, those who are around us, and the one who is with us. The fruit of the Spirit in our lives effects blessings to God, beneficence to our fellow creatures, and benefits to ourselves.

The third particular about the fruit of the Spirit that is regularly pointed out by writers and speakers is that it is a supernatural work of the Holy Spirit in and through the believer and not an acceleration of the individual's natural temperament or disposition. While it is obvious that some persons are more loving and expressive of that love than are others, that is not a fruit of the Spirit, for this same factor can be observed in the animal kingdom. Similarly, some children seem to be born with a calm, peaceful disposition, while others are contentious and almost warlike from day one, but the first is not displaying the fruit of the Spirit any more than the second is evidencing an absence of that fruit; each is displaying a natural temperament.

The fruit described in Galatians 5 is not a pattern for Christians to follow in changing their lives; it is a description of what the Holy Spirit will produce in the lives of those who will put to death the works of their fleshly natures and submit to the inner workings of the Spirit. Matthew Henry comments:

> If we would approve ourselves to be Christ's we must make it our constant care to crucify the flesh. Christ will never own those as his who yield themselves the servants of sin. It is not enough that we cease to do evil, but we must learn to do well. Our Christianity obliges us not only to oppose the works of the flesh, but to bring forth the fruits of the Spirit too.

The Christian does not produce this fruit; he bears it. It is not a human endeavor aided by the Spirit but is a divine enablement submitted to by Christian believers. Each may bear all of the fruit, but none can produce any of it.

Seldom do I find believers who have a problem with this truth. We know we cannot produce *agape* (divine love), nor are we capable of synthesizing divine joy or peace, and our inherent long-suffering, gentleness, and goodness will never meet the standards of the Word of God. We are all too happy to admit that apart from a genuine and progressive work of the Spirit we cannot manifest these qualities. We accept the fruit of the Spirit to be a work of the Spirit in us rather than a work of our will on behalf of the Spirit, with only one exception: *faith*. Somehow we still think that we can and must produce this one grape on the cluster. As Dr. Charles Price declared many years ago, "To many, many Christians, faith is still their own ability to believe a promise or a truth, and is often based on their struggles to drive away doubt and unbelief through a process of continuous affirmations."

If we can produce faith, why is it listed as a segment of the fruit of the Spirit? Perhaps this is why some translators and commentators chose to change the consistent meaning of the word *pistis* (faith) to *pistos* (faithfulness). Isn't this putting the cart before the horse? Faith is the force; faithfulness is the flow. Faith is the action, while faithfulness is the reaction. We need to guard lest we seek to produce the cause instead of the effect, for faith is the cause, and our faithfulness, fidelity, or trustfulness is but an effect of that faith. Whenever we try to produce what only God can produce, we will meet with frustration and failure.

Surely it is not by accident that of the multitude of titles given to Christ in the Old Testament, He conferred only one of them upon New Testament believers. Ten times the prophets called the coming Messiah the Branch, and before His Crucifixion Jesus told His disciples, "I am the vine, ye are the branches: He that abideth in me, and I in him, the same bringeth forth much fruit: for without me ye can do nothing" (John 15:5). In conferring the title of the Branch upon believers, Jesus coupled the necessity of an abiding relationship with the production of fruit. A severed branch can do nothing but wither and die, but an abiding branch will not only live but be fruit bearing. The life force originates in the vine, not in the branch. The genetic strain, the growth cycle, the timing of fruit production, and the very nature of the fruit is locked in the established plant, not in the extended branches. The life is in Christ; the nature of the fruit is in Jesus, and the production of that fruit is controlled by Him. We, the branches, have little more responsibility than to remain integrally united to the vine and to allow its life forces to flow through and produce fruit within and upon us.

Faith is a part of this divine flow. The fruit of the Spirit (which includes divine faith) does not spring from anything inherent within us, but is the result of this new life flowing through us by the Holy Spirit. It is not a product of our minds or emotions; it is a result of the presence of the Third Person of the Trinity within our lives. We need only remain in an intimate, abiding connection with Christ Jesus our Lord to enjoy a production of faith.

The fruit of the Spirit is an immediate demonstration of life, for none would call a producing vineyard dead, and even the most critical cynic is taken aback when the living fruit of the Spirit is evidenced in the life of a believer, since an argument is no match for demonstratable experience.

Fresh, ripe, aromatic fruit has a way of stirring the gastric juices in the stomach and creating an appetite. Furthermore, since fruit is not ingested by the plant but is grown for consumption by those who cannot produce fruit, others get their first taste of the divine realm from association with fruit-bearing Christians. Our freshly ripened faith creates a hunger, and fortunately the same fruit that creates hunger can satisfy that hunger.

The purpose of the *fruit* of the Spirit is different, of course, than the purpose of the *gifts* of the Spirit. We may speak of the *gifts* of the Spirit as a *work* of the Spirit *through* the individual, while the *fruit* of the Spirit is a production *in* that individual. The operation of the gifts of the Spirit is the direct result of the Spirit's active energy, while the fruit is the outcome of His indwelling presence. We might even say that faith as a fruit is passive, while faith as a gift is active; but we'll examine that far more closely in the next chapter.

12
Faith and Gifts

Dr. Charles Price was very fond of saying, "Faith is one of two things. It is either a gift of God, or a fruit of the Spirit." If he was right, then faith is either being developed within us by the Spirit or imparted unto us by God. Having already looked at faith as a fruit, let's turn our attention to faith as a gift.

There is a broad and a narrow sense in which faith may be viewed as a gift. In a general way, all faith, even natural faith, has its ultimate origins in God and has come to us as a gift from God. In a more specific way, however, faith is listed as one of the nine special energized operations of the Spirit through individuals in the Church.

To the church at Rome, Paul wrote ". . . God hath dealt to every man the measure of faith" (Romans 12:3). Commenting on this, Dr. Price wrote:

> Faith is measured in the scales of God, even as we measure the commodities of earth. More than once our blessed Lord talked about little faith and great faith. He mentioned weak faith and strong faith. As we need the gift or fruit of faith, it is imparted by the Lord, in order that *God's will, rather than ours,* will be done on earth, and in us, even as it is in Heaven. There are many times when *our desires* are contrary to the will of God. Many times in our ignorance we would do the thing which would bring sorrow instead of joy. If we possessed the faith, for use at any and all

times to bring about our own desires, it is clearly to be seen
that the results would be disastrous.

While working on this book I enjoyed monitoring a special
class being taught by the Reverend Dick Mills during a convention at which both of us were speakers. He mentioned
this passage in Romans about God's giving a measure of faith
to everyone, and said that when a small measure of faith is
given, it is all that is needed by that individual. Others, because of their personalities or deep doubts, need the touch,
excitement, and demonstration that will undergird them
until faith can more fully mature in them. But, he assured
us, God will always give a measure sufficient to get us
through to ultimate victory. Hallelujah!

The measure given is the measure needed. If another
seems to have received a larger proportion of faith, it is because he needs more than you, for God faithfully deals to
every individual the measure of faith needed to walk in harmony with the divine will. Beyond that point, faith will not
be imparted.

Dick Mills shared a simple illustration with me. In a vision
a pastor petitioned the Lord to specially bless three of the
outstanding saints in his congregation. Jesus agreed to do so,
and as the three stood by the altar at the front of the church,
Jesus walked by the first saint, stood near the second, and
reached out to touch the third.

"This third Christian must have great faith," the pastor
said.

"No," Jesus answered. "The first person sensed My presence the moment I walked into the room. The second needed
the nearness of My presence, but this third person had to be
touched by Me to unlock faith in My presence."

The measure of faith given was commensurate with the

need. Every allotment of faith is, generally speaking, a gift of God. However, since faith is a *gift* of God, we do not possess it to use at will, but for the purpose for which God gives it and permits us to keep it. As Dr. Price would say, "We trust Him when faith is withheld, and praise Him when it is given."

But I am far more concerned in this chapter with the specific gift of faith as taught to the church at Corinth. "Now concerning spiritual gifts, brethren, I would not have you ignorant. . . . For to one is given by the Spirit the word of wisdom; to another the word of knowledge by the same Spirit; To another faith by the same Spirit . . ." (1 Corinthians 12:1, 8, 9), Paul wrote.

In this list of nine charismatas, or "special abilities," as Ken Taylor translates it, are three classes of gifts with three gifts in each. The first group of three supernaturally enables a person to know—word of wisdom, word of knowledge, and discerning of spirits. The second group supernaturally enables the possessor to do—faith, working of miracles, and gifts of healing—while the third group supernaturally enables the believer to speak—prophecy, tongues, and interpretation of tongues.

The third gift of the Spirit to be mentioned in Paul's list is *faith*. This is an operation of faith that is specifically special and supremely supernatural. It is as far beyond "natural" faith as a "word of wisdom" is beyond a secular education. It is much more than a divine energizing of a natural endowment, just as a "gift of healing" is more than the art of a skillful surgeon. There is the natural ability and there is also the spiritual enablement, but in this listing of the charismata of the Holy Spirit we are directed to thoughts, actions, and speech that are far beyond the native ability of any person. It is a work of God's Spirit.

In listing *faith* among these special abilities Paul is unveiling the availability of a realm of faith that is beyond our capacity to contain, and is often beyond our ability to conceive. It is supernatural faith, or as Weymouth translates it, "special faith."

When we view faith as a fruit, we see evidence of divine life in that fruit, but when we view faith as a gift, we see the effect of that life in the operation of the gift. Faith as a fruit edifies the individual, while faith as a gift edifies the entire body of Christ where it is exercised. Similarly, faith as a fruit functions as an inward principle, while faith as a gift functions more as an outward power. We might even say that faith as a fruit is concerned with Christian character, while faith as a gift is concerned with Christ-like capability.

In Harold Horton's small book *The Gifts of the Spirit,* he lists nine scriptural uses of the gift of faith. Without using the space it would require to list the Bible illustrations he gives, let me quote his nine purposes, for though they are not exhaustive they are beautifully illustrative.

1. The Gift of Faith was employed for direct supernatural blessing in fulfillment of human utterance.
2. For personal protection in perilous circumstances.
3. For supernatural sustenance in famine or fasting.
4. For receiving the astounding promises of God.
5. For administering spiritual correction to gross offenders.
6. For supernatural victory in the fight.
7. To assist in domestic and industrial problems.
8. To raise the dead.
9. Finally, Faith is the Gift employed in casting out evil spirits.

While the above list is far too small to adequately illustrate the operation of the gift of faith, it does help us realize why some expositors refer to it as "miracle faith," while Weymouth translates it "special faith," Coneybeare calls it "wonder working faith," and Meyers translates it "heroic faith." It is faith that reaches beyond the borders of our world and brings supernatural protection, provision, and power to bear on our human limitations and problems. This gift of faith is a work of the Spirit that enables the saint to receive, not perform, miracles.

Of course we realize that faith undergirds the operation of every gift of the Spirit, but it is unfair to say that the *gift* of faith is the basis of the other gifts, although, admittedly, it may often operate in conjunction with the other gifts. Since faith's operation is less spectacular than that of any other gift, being manifested often secretly, silently, and over longer periods of time, it is often overlooked. But mountain-moving, tree-withering, demon-casting-out faith is an operation of the gift of faith. It is "special faith" in the highest sense of the word *special.*

For Peter to sleep chained to a Roman guard while awaiting execution (*see* Acts 12:6), and for Paul to encourage the fearful sailors to eat food in the midst of a storm that eventually destroyed their boat (*see* Acts 27:35, 36) required a working of *special faith,* a gift of faith. Paul repeatedly faced frenzied mobs of people, withstood learned accusers in religious and secular courts, and survived many physical beatings by operation of this gift. This gift of faith was an energizer to Paul and an enigma to his persecutors. They could not see, feel, or know what he knew, for it was supernaturally operating in Paul, but they eventually saw the results of this gift of faith as believers were raised up in all the areas where Paul was so seriously threatened. This gift of faith not only preserved Paul, it presented the claims of the Gospel of Christ with such authority that lives were changed, believers were strengthened, and even kings and rulers were moved favorably toward the Gospel.

The gift of faith operates by the direct intervention of the Holy Spirit. It has neither its origins nor its initiation in the attitudes of the believer. Sometimes it is a *rhema* sentence or word, or perhaps a promise that God isolates for us, that brings an operation of the gift of faith. No other operation of faith is more dependent upon receiving a *rhema* word from God, and those who enjoy such a hearing of God's voice have learned to keep themselves full of the *logos* (the written word) to be prepared to receive a spoken word, since God does not operate apart from His revealed Word.

Other times this gift of faith begins to function totally independent from any other source of stimulation or communication. The believer just has a supernatural knowing, awareness, and confidence that are far beyond his natural faith limits.

This gift of faith may take the form of an inner illumination, an active assurance, a continuing calmness, or a pulsating power, and it will give the participant a physical or emotional evidence of its presence. It is generally accompanied by inner peace, calmness, and tranquility. It is very much like the eye of the hurricane—calmness in the midst of a devastating storm. When the gift of faith is functioning, the believer is as assured of a change in the situation as though it had already transpired, although there may be a lengthy time delay between the operation of the gift and the actualization of that gift. This level of faith knows *that* it knows, and knows *what* it knows, but often is hard pressed to explain *why* it knows. But it is not a leap in the dark, or a crawling out on a limb; it is a moving in perfect harmony with the will of God even though that will is still an unexplained factor. While it may not know the facts, it knows God and has an inner assurance from Him that everything is under divine control.

Osward Chambers said, "Faith by its very nature must be tried, and the real trial of faith is not that we find it difficult to trust God, but that God's character has to be cleared in our own minds. . . . Faith in the Bible is faith in God against everything that contradicts Him—I will remain true to God's character whatever He may do. 'Though He slay me, yet will I trust Him'—this is the most sublime utterance of faith in the whole of the Bible."

Somewhere in our life of faith we must learn that God Himself is the object of all our faith. We are urged to maintain "the steadfastness of your *faith in Christ*" (Colossians 2:5, italics added). Consider with me what is involved in having God as the object as well as the source of our faith.

13
Faith in God

Many years ago, Dr. Thomas Arnold wrote in *Homiletic Commentary: Hebrews:*

> Every one knows how much the word "faith" has to do with Christianity. The word is, indeed, peculiar to religion, and in an especial manner peculiar to the religion of Christ. In His revelation to man God has taken hold of that one part of our nature which was lying most neglected, and yet in which the seed of our highest perfection is alone to be found. Faith is indeed that which most raises us from a state of brute selfishness and brute ignorance; and leading us on gradually, according to our gradual growth, from one high object to another, ends by offering to the mind of the Christian the most perfect object of all, even God Himself, our Father and Saviour and Sanctifier.

It is the failure to see that the ultimate object of our faith is God Himself which causes many to prostitute their faith rather than progress in it. The measurement of faith is not only its strength but its object. It is possible to have faith in faith. Some have almost deified faith itself, believing that their faith can do all things, provide all things, and solve all mysteries. Perhaps the resurgence of ascribing God-like qualities to faith instead of letting faith bring us to God in this twentieth century is America's nearly wholesale embracing of the philosophy of humanism, which puts man at the center of all things instead of God. Whenever we espouse the deity of man, we automatically forsake the deity of God; hence we subconsciously think of faith as a possessed force that will, of itself, produce or perform whatever we direct it to do, instead of seeing it as a channel to bring us into a walk with God Who, the Scriptures affirm, is to be the object of our faith.

If we do not heed the testimony of the early apostles that we must have ". . . repentance toward God, and faith toward our Lord Jesus Christ" (Acts 20:21), we may fall into the trap of having faith in formulas more than having faith in God and His Word. Our scientifically minded society is formula oriented, and we love to bring the exactness of mathematical equations into our religious experiences. We find ourselves dealing with phrases, texts (sometimes out of context), clichés, and specific recipes in preference to dealing with the living God. But it is not formula but faith which pleases God. God sometimes follows a known formula, but oftentimes, in His omniscience, He functions beyond our limited, finite understanding of His principles, power, and purposes.

When we shift the focus of our faith from God to anything else, we tend to think and exercise faith *for* rather than faith *in*. Faith *for* makes us things oriented instead of God oriented. With a "faith *for*" mentality we become the source; possessions become the object, and faith is viewed as the force that brings the desired thing, or end, into our experience. Actually we unwittingly seek to become the creators rather than the creatures who have access to the Creator.

God's ultimate purpose in giving us faith was to make us dependent upon God, not independent from Him. Abraham's faith was not for a land but in a speaking God Who walked with him out of Ur into Canaan. Faith is given to make the heavenly realm real and available to us, not to make us self-sufficient apart from God's domain.

Repeatedly the New Testament speaks of our faith *in* God or *in* the Lord Jesus. God is the accepted and expected object of our faith. Faith has been imparted to man to bring him to God, for God made man for intimate fellowship, union, and communion with Himself. Although sin separated man from God, salvation reunited the creature with his Creator, and faith is the divine channel of both that salvation and that companionship.

When Paul found it necessary to write about his pedigree he added, "But what things were gain to me, those I counted loss for Christ. Yea doubtless, and I count all things but loss for the excellency of the knowledge of Christ Jesus my Lord . . . that I may win Christ, And be found in Him. . . . That I may know him . . ." (Philippians 3:7–10). Paul's desire was for neither position nor possession, and not even for faith. His yearning, burning passion was for realization of and relationship with Jesus Christ. Knowing God was paramount on Paul's priority list. Motivating, manipulating, or moving God on his behalf did not enter into Paul's use of faith, for God the Father, God the Son, and God the Holy Spirit were the consistent objects of his faith. Dare we content ourselves with a lesser knowing? Is it satisfying to God for us to be enamored with the power of faith and what it will produce rather than to be deeply in love with God, the true source and object of our faith?

Without faith God can be neither appreciated nor apprehended, "for he that cometh to God must believe that he is, and that he is a rewarder of them that diligently seek him" (Hebrews 11:6). God cannot be discovered by man; He must be revealed to man, and faith is the vital key that unlocks the door to the knowledge of God. To seek God apart from faith is to seek in vain, but "ye shall seek me, and find me, when ye shall search for me with all your heart" (Jeremiah 29:13). The search that finds God is the search of the heart, and faith is a matter of the heart, not of the head. Faith, when released from our restraints, ascends toward God's presence as naturally as a gas-filled balloon rises when its string is released. Perhaps if we would cease grasping our faith so tightly and just relax in the faith that God has given to us, we would find ourselves being lofted into His presence.

Faith in God's Person will always involve faith in God's promises, for God and His Word are inseparable, as John expresses: "In the beginning was the Word, and the Word was with God, and the Word was God" (John 1:1). Faith is the force that not only enables us to believe the veracity of God's promises but also helps us grasp them and bring them into fulfillment in our lives. To know the Word and to believe that it is actually the Word of God does not change either our condition or our circumstances. We need to mix faith with the promises to effect the desired result.

Peter addressed his second epistle to "them that have obtained like precious faith with us" (2 Peter 1:1), and then he assures us that God's "divine power hath given unto us all things that pertain unto life and godliness, through the knowledge of him that hath called us to glory and virtue: Whereby are given unto us exceeding great and precious promises: that by these ye might be partakers of the divine nature ..." (2 Peter 1:3, 4). Knowing God to the point of being a partaker of His nature requires a faith involvement with His promises.

This will not be a faith in the promises separate from faith in God but in conjunction with our faith in God. It is "being fully persuaded that, what he had promised, he was able also to perform" (Romans 4:21). The validity of any promise is based on the veracity of the one who made that

promise, and when we have ascended in faith into a knowledge and relationship with God, we have complete confidence in His promises because we have complete confidence
in His Person. "God is not a man, that he should lie; neither
the son of man, that he should repent: hath he said, and shall
he not do it? or hath he spoken, and shall he not make it
good?" (Numbers 23:19).

The hymnist puts it:

'Tis so sweet to trust in Jesus, just to take Him at His
    Word;
Just to rest upon His promise; Just to know thus saith the
    Lord.

When faith's object is God, it will also envelop God's
power. When Peter and John explained the miraculous
healing of the lame man at the temple's Gate Beautiful, they
preached Jesus, declaring, "And his name through faith in
his name hath made this man strong, whom ye see and
know: yea, the faith which is by him hath given him this
perfect soundness in the presence of you all" (Acts 3:16).

When God is known His power is shown. It may be difficult to develop faith in the power of God apart from a
knowing of God, but those who know God best easily find
faith for His demonstrative power. Knowing Him will involve knowing what He can do, and once there is an assurance that He desires to do it, faith readily grasps the exercise
of power as a natural extension of God's Person and promises. To really know God as omnipotent is to never be surprised at a display of that omnipotence.

The saint who has channeled faith directly to God's Person will find that faith *in* God involves faith not only in
God's promises and power, but also in God's provision. That

God is able to do is one thing; that God has provided to do is still another. Israel lived for forty years on God's provision of manna, not His promise of manna or His demonstrated ability to produce that manna. God, our loving heavenly Father, has made lavish provision for His children. There need be no lacking of any good thing, nor need there be exertion of great pleadings or spiritual energy to be the beneficiary of these provisions. When seated at Father's table you merely say, "Pass the potatoes, please." They are there as His provision, so "Ask, and it shall be given you ..." (Matthew 7:7).

Faith for provision, apart from faith in God's Person, becomes most difficult, since Christ Jesus is God's provision for His people. "I am the way ...," He testified (John 14:6). "But of him are ye in Christ Jesus, who of God is made unto us wisdom, and righteousness, and sanctification, and redemption: That, according as it is written, He that glorieth, let him glory in the Lord" (1 Corinthians 1:30, 31). God has not provided for us apart from Himself; hence unfeigned faith will not be an intelligent understanding but a deliberate commitment to a Person. Faith involves us with a Person, not an impersonal power.

Oswald Chambers said, "Faith never knows where it is being led, but it loves and knows the One Who is leading. It is a life of *faith,* not of intellect and reason, but a life of knowing Who makes us 'go'." If my wife goes on a trip by herself, she seeks money for her ticket, food, and lodging, but if she goes with me, she just naturally expects me to be her source of provision and merely stays close to me at mealtimes. Should it be any less in our relation with God?

When unfeigned faith finds its object in the Person of God Himself, the one in whom faith is found will begin to embrace God's purposes for his life. If God is Who He says He is, and keeps His promises with unlimited power and unstinted provisions, then it should not be difficult to believe that His purposes are better than our purposes. His goals for our lives are superior to our goals, and we can pray confidently that "Thy will be done in earth, as it is in heaven" (Matthew 6:10). God is still in control of His heaven, His earth, and His hell and all of their inhabitants. I may not understand that control, but faith accepts God's statement that He is, in fact, in control of all things including my personal life. Therefore, I need not wrestle with God by exerting great faith; I can rest in God because of faith's assurance that God's purposes are fully being served right here in the nasty here-and-now.

Because faith is such a powerful spiritual force, God usually restricts the measure of faith any person can exercise until He Himself has become the object of that faith; then, often, He begins to unfold the highest level of faith in His entire economy: God's faith! What could we do if we could actually be possessors of and channels for God's own personal, unlimited, omnipotent faith? Jesus gave His disciples some insight into this potentiality when He said, "Have the faith *of* God" (Mark 11:22, marginal reading); but that truth will have to be developed in the next chapter.

14
Faith of God

Faith is so rare and so precious that it is the first thing Jesus will look for when He comes again (*see* Luke 18:8). It is a commodity so vital that it is impossible to please God without it (*see* Hebrews 11:6). It is the lifeline between heaven and earth without which the Christian would not long survive (*see* Galatians 2:20), and both its founding and its fulfillment are the Lord Jesus Christ (*see* Hebrews 12:2).

Faith is not a mere attitude or a simple act; as a matter of fact, faith is a complex, many-faceted heavenly gem, whose full beauty will never be appreciated if viewed from only one perspective. In order to mentally visualize the varied factors in faith, we may help ourselves by loosely defining different *aspects* of faith, taking care not to think in terms of different *kinds* of faith; for actually faith is faith is faith, just as electricity is electricity is electricity. But we have differing forms of electricity, different voltages, various amperages, and variant ways of transmitting that amazing power. So it is with faith. While faith is a power as real in the spirit world as electricity is real in our natural world, its form is alterable, and its accomplishment is determined more by the nature of the channel through which it is released than by its inherent nature.

Simplistically we could say that there is natural faith and divine faith: faith that has its origins in man and faith that has its origins in God. All men have faith. The farmer would never plow the soil if he didn't have faith for a harvest. But not all men have divine faith, for while natural faith is a thing of the head, divine faith is a thing of the heart. Even the demons have the head faith (natural faith), for they believe the reality of God and the veracity of His Word and tremble (*see* James 2:19), but this is not redemptive for them. Saving faith is not a matter of the head; it is an energy in the heart, for "The word is nigh thee, even in thy mouth, *and in thy heart:* that is, the word of faith. . . . For with the heart man believeth unto righteousness . . ." (Romans 10:8, 10, italics added).

But God has not revealed faith to be utterly simplistic. There is natural faith, divine faith, and saving faith, but beyond this there is what we could call "basic" or "general" faith. It is the energy by which we live the Christian life, love our faithful God, obey the written Word, and minister in the earthly Church. This "general faith" can be passive or very active. It is the foundation spoken of in the introduction to the eleventh chapter of Hebrews. Usually Christians have this "basic" faith in mind when they speak of *faith.* It is the normative definition of faith, and is often spoken of as *our* faith.

Beyond these aspects of faith, however, we have also seen faith as a fruit and faith as a gift—the first dealing with our character, and the second dealing with our competence. Faith develops silently as a result of an abiding relationship, and faith also develops charismatically as a result of a special energizing of God's Holy Spirit.

Nevertheless, even viewing the facets of natural, saving, "basic" faith, faith as a fruit, and the gift of faith does not give a complete representation of faith. There is also the major aspect of divine faith to be considered, for although all but "natural faith" have their origins in God, there is a form of faith that is merely called the "faith *of* God." Jesus challenged His disciples to "Have the faith of God" (Mark 11:22, marginal reading). Admittedly most translators have chosen to say "faith in God," but in the Greek, "God" is in the genitive case, which allows either translation with equal justification. The issue lies in whether God is the object of the faith or the subject of that faith (where it is possessive and represents God's own faith). Obviously, the context must determine the issue, and in the verses surrounding this text Jesus had cursed the fruitless fig tree, which withered and died overnight. When the amazed disciples marveled at this miracle, Jesus said, "Have the faith of God," and then proceeded to explain to them that when God's own faith was operating through them they could cast literal mountains into the sea with a verbal command (*see* Mark 11:20–24).

In his outstanding book *From the Pinnacle of the Temple,* Dr. Charles Farah, Jr., who has been a professor of theological and historical studies at Oral Roberts University since 1967, says:

> Since we have previously shown this to be most likely a subjective rather than an objective genitive: that is, that God is the subject and author of faith and that it is His kind of faith, we might better translate this, "have the faith of God" or "have God-like faith" or "have God's faith." All would catch the substance of the idea.

Paul seemed to grasp this concept, for he wrote: "I am crucified with Christ: nevertheless I live; yet not I, but Christ liveth in me: and the life which I now live in the flesh I live by the faith of the Son of God, who loved me, and gave himself for me" (Galatians 2:20). Paul clearly testified that he did not live, move, minister, and function in *his* faith but in the "faith of the Son of God." Paul had learned to lay hold of God's faith as the energy and force of his life. Everything

that issued from his carnal nature had been crucified with
Christ, and in exchange he lived a quickened life sustained
and energized by God's own faith. What a glorious exchange: Christ's life for ours; His faith for ours; and His love
for ours.

How great this level of faith must be!—"God-like faith."
Imagine having access to the unlimited, unwavering, inex-
haustible faith of God. It was that faith that spoke the worlds
into existence; formed man out of the dust of the earth; and
continues to control everything He has created. "Have God's
faith" must have been a command beyond the disciples'
mental comprehension or volitional ability to respond.

Or was it so much a command as a commitment? When
Christ says "Have . . ." it is an offering of a gift, similar to
our saying "Have a mint" as we stretch forth our hand to
make the candy available to the recipient. "Have the faith of
God" is an offering of that limitless faith. Jesus had it, Paul
had it, and we, too, may have it, for Jesus is ". . . the author
and finisher of our faith . . ." (Hebrews 12:2), or, as the New
International Version translates it, "Let us fix our eyes on
Jesus, the Pioneer [footnote: Originator] and Perfecter of our
faith. . . ." Jesus is the Author, the Pioneer, the Originator of
our faith. The faith *of* God does not have its origin in the be-
liefs of man but in the very nature of God Himself. It begins
and ends in Him, so nothing we can do will manufacture it;
it must be imparted by Him.

How puny our little weak human faith looks when it is
laid alongside God's almighty faith, but as sad as that comparison may be, consider how tragic it is when that impotent
faith is labeled as divine faith. The difference in the faiths is
not the label but the source. That which originates in God is
divine faith, and that which originates in man is human
faith no matter what the label may read.

The faith *of* God must come from God. He is its only source, and He has an eternal monopoly on its distribution. It cannot be synthesized or counterfeited. It cannot be purchased or bargained for. It is never given as a reward, and its formula remains forever the secret of God. Man's participation in this faith is by the grace of God as He imparts it as a free gift. It does not come as the result of fasting and prayer, nor can any form of religious incantations bring it into the midst of a congregation of people. It is totally God's faith as to origin, transmission, conduct, and control.

When by God's sovereign grace the faith *of* God begins to manifest itself through a believer, it does not become a resident gift, nor is that individual given the liberty to use the faith according to his or her will. God, Who imparts this faith, also directs its operation. We are the channels for its flow but not the controllers of that flow, for the same limitation that makes it impossible for a human to produce a divine force makes it dangerous for that human to have the control of a divine force. God imparts His faith for a specific purpose and then withdraws it from man's grasp. Leaving it resident with men would be as dangerous as allowing a two-year-old to have a loaded pistol among his playthings.

It is God's faith, His impartation, and His control of that imparted faith, but it is amazingly productive. His faith parted the Red Sea, opened the earth to swallow Korah, and rained daily manna upon Israel. God's faith cleansed the lepers, opened blinded eyes, and raised the dead. This divine faith is capable of doing anything and everything that God decrees, for, as Dr. Charles Price says, *"You can't have faith without results any more than you can have motion without movement."* Since this is God's faith it will have God's results, and they are always tremendous by man's estimation.

"Have the faith *of* God" (Mark 11:22, marginal reading) is

a commitment that requires an impartation. It is not achieved; it is received. When Paul wrote to the Roman church, he said, "I long to see you, that I may impart unto you some spiritual gift, to the end ye may be established" (Romans 1:11). Paul recognized his inability to impart until he was in their presence. Impartation is not information that can be transmitted by letter. Impartation is an infusion from one to another when in close proximity to each other. To have God's faith, then, will require spending time in God's presence. He does not communicate this faith through His Word; He infuses it into us by His presence.

If we have mountains to move, then we would do well to stop examining the mountains, call off the surveyors, and spend our time and energy getting in and staying in His presence. That was where David received new faith when it seemed that everything had failed. That is where Paul and Silas received new faith when jailed at Philippi, and that is where we will obtain a new, energetic, dynamic, totally supernatural faith.

How we need to lift our eyes above the needs to the Need-Meeter. We need to shift our gaze from the faith to the God of that faith, for we need the Energizer far more than we need His energy. The true issue is not our relationship to things, needs, believing, confession, or even our faith, but our relationship to God Himself. The closer and warmer that relationship becomes, the greater the availability of God's faith will be.

We cannot function without faith, and we cannot successfully produce divine faith, so we can either find God to receive His faith, or we can fake it. We can accept His divine energy or act as though we have it. We may live in faith with all of its correlatives, or we can pretend we have faith and contend the rest of our lives with the contrarieties to faith.

SECTION II

Feigned Faith and Its Contrarieties to Faith

Interlude
Contrarieties to Faith

While awaiting such changes as are necessary for scene 2, let's review what we learned about *unfeigned faith.* Wuest translates 2 Timothy 1:5, "Having been reminded of the un-hypocritical faith which is in you, which is of such a nature as to have been at home first in your grandmother Lois and in Eunice your mother, and is now, I am convinced, in you as well."

The Greek word for "unfeigned" is actually two words combined: *a,* meaning "not," and *hupokritos,* meaning "an actor." So, as Dick Mills told us, *"Unfeigned faith* is faith without pretense, faith without a mask, without putting on an act, or merely reciting dialogue as though you're reading a script." If the negative (*a*) is dropped, we have *feigned faith,* faith that is playacting, or, as William Hendriksen says, "a vile conceit in pompous words expressed."

In *Black's New Testament Commentary,* J. N. Kelly says, "It has been objected that Paul could never have qualified faith as sincere. He can speak of sincere love in Romans 12:9 despite the fact that love which is insincere is no more 'love' than insincere faith is the genuine article (faith). The point is that, while faith itself cannot be insincere, it is possible to deceive oneself or others that one possesses it."

In W. E. Vine's *Commentary on Timothy and Titus,* the author says of unfeigned faith, "It marks the absence of everything that is contrary to what is genuine and true." Conversely, then, feigned faith would mark the presence of everything that is contrary to what is genuine and true faith. It would be a faith which is an empty profession, an easy assent to formulas, lacking the vital principle of uniting one to a living Christ.

If *feigned* is hypocritical, insincere, playing the actor, then it is not genuinely from the heart; it is mere lip-faith, mental assent, or projection of positive attitudes.

Every true is challenged by a false, and every real has its threatening counterfeit. Faith is no exception. There are religious opportunists and charlatans who pretend to have divine faith in order to merchandise human need and suffering. These unbelieving ones are already damned to the lake of fire (*see* Revelation 21:8).

Far sadder is the plight of well-intentioned persons who somehow grasp wrong concepts and accept the title of "faith" for them. They have the desire and the right vocabulary, but what results is a far cry from divine faith.

Often they are very formula oriented and possess great religious zeal, but the very nature of the contrariety that they have embraced guarantees that they will never function in faith unless God in His great mercy saves them from their feigned, false, hypocritical substitute and grants unto them a new measure of faith.

This, of course, is among the divine purposes for the coming of Christ Jesus. But none will be delivered from the false until he recognizes it as counterfeit.

In section II we want to examine feigned faith and its contrarieties to faith, seeking to discover the oppositeness and opposition to faith. What is faith's antithesis? What forces work against true faith, and what attitudes and expressions indicate an actor at work rather than a saint in believing? If we can ascertain these, we can better isolate the false and embrace the true faith which comes from the very heart of God.

15

Faith Versus Fear

The agnostic likes to point out the seeming contradictions to be seen in the Scriptures, such as this contrast between a command and a commitment: ". . . pass the time of your sojourning here in fear," and, "For God hath not given us the spirit of fear . . ." (1 Peter 1:17; 2 Timothy 1:7). Is one passage a contravention of the other? Or are these two weights in the balance scales of truth?

Similarly, John tells us, "There is no fear in love; but perfect love casteth out fear . . ." (1 John 4:18), while Paul says, ". . . let us serve God with thankfulness in the ways which please Him, but always with reverence and holy fear" (Hebrews 12:28 PHILLIPS).

Fear is both a prerequisite to faith and a deterrent of faith. The "fear of the Lord" is one of the dominating thoughts of the Old Testament and is supported by the New Testament. Fear must be recognized as one of the basic responses to God's demand on men. Actually, fear is tantamount to religion, for the very essence of religion is a form of fear produced by the realization of the being and nature of God. It grows from pondering over the character and nature of God, for it is God's purity which fills man with a sense of his own unworthiness. This fear of the Lord is a permanent element in man's relation to God, but this form of the emotion should more properly be called "awe" or "reverence."

To fear God is to obey and worship Him. The person

whose concept of God has brought him to a holy reverence will cease giving orders to God and will take orders instead. It is only one who has never seen the majesty, dominion, and holy nature of God who will grasp at faith as an Aladdin's lamp empowering him to make a genie out of God.

Not only is "the fear of the Lord . . . the beginning of wisdom" (Psalms 111:10), but Godly fear is the beginning of a relationship with God out of which true faith can flow. This fear-inspired relationship is absolutely essential both for obtaining and maintaining living faith. We must see Him, serve Him, fear Him, and love Him to be enabled by Him. Faith is not a faucet to be turned on and off at man's will; it is a flow of the very nature of God Himself and comes out of intimate relationship with God.

This fear of the Lord, this divine awe, is God's answer to man's anxiety, his uneasy conscience, and his divided loyalties. Properly submitted to, it transforms man's anxiety about himself and his world, leaving him with only this one fear, which is a trembling adoration of the transcendent Holy Lord. Too frequently, however, this noble form of fear degenerates as the true nature of God is less and less clearly understood, and it becomes a paralyzing sense of terror. Instead of fearing God, as we are commanded, we fear ourselves, our circumstances, our future, and our declared spiritual enemy, the devil.

This deteriorated form of faith was graphically evidenced by the disciples when the evening storm nearly swamped the boat in which Jesus was soundly sleeping. Fearfully awakening Him and charging Him with unconcern over their plight, they were astounded at His authority in calming the wind and the waves, and they exclaimed one to another, "What manner of man is this . . ." (Matthew 8:27). If they had but known "what manner of man is this," they would have taken a nap with Him instead of submitting their hearts to terror. Terrorizing fear in the life of the believer is always a result of a lack of the true "fear of the Lord." Our weak, limited knowledge of His nature causes us to think that circumstances are out of His control, and that maybe the devil has some almightiness after all.

Whenever we turn our attention from knowing God in our endeavors to live a life of faith, we open ourselves to this immobilizing force called fear. And faster than we would have believed possible, we discover that this fear has stopped sound thinking, exaggerated our difficulties, murmured at Christian duties, and even blamed God for the bitterness of soul and spirit that remain as a residue of faith.

Fear is devastating. Fear excites the emotions, dulls the senses, confuses the reasoning, and greatly amplifies anxiety. Fear is paralyzing, terrorizing, demoralizing, and anesthetizing. It destroys logical thinking, faith, hope, morality, self-respect, and, if given enough rein, it will destroy the life, for fear is responsible for illness and disease, insanity, depravity, and much suicide.

Despair and dismay are the final products of fear. Fear of giants in the land caused Israel to wander for thirty-eight years and finally accept death in the desert rather than obey God in entering the Promised Land.

Much fear masquerades under the guise of worry. "I'm not afraid, but I am a little worried" is a frequently heard remark. Yet worry is little more than fear unexpressed, and it is seldom warranted or worthy of the energy expended on it. After checking case histories over a period of several years, a group of psychologists developed a "worry table." They reported the following reasons for worry: (1) worries about disasters which, as later events proved, never happened, 40 percent; (2) worries about decisions in the past that cannot be recalled or remedied, 30 percent; (3) worries about possible sickness that never came, 12 percent; (4) worries about children and friends, 10 percent; and (5) worries that have no real foundation, 8 percent. Eighty-eight percent of their worries were groundless, fruitless, and futile.

Nonetheless, this apprehensive fear of the uncontrollable can cause strong reaction in the nature of man. The feeling of extreme helplessness frustrates him. The imagined urgency of the issue drives him to action, but it is action he is emotionally unable to perform rationally. Fear becomes a bottled-up force in a person, which begins to do a destructive work within him in spite of himself. It is much like the drunken man fearfully fighting the reflected image of himself in the mirror. Fear makes us our own worst enemy.

It should be obvious to all of us that fear and faith will not mix. As a matter of fact, fear is the exact opposite of faith; it is faith flowing in the opposite direction. Fear says, "It won't be done," while faith says, "It shall be done." Not one of us can be filled with anxiety over tomorrow and still be filled with confidence in the God Who holds tomorrow. The energy that once flowed to God as trust is now flowing to negative circumstances as terror.

Fear and faith are diametrically opposed to each other. Fear deprives man of his reason, while faith gives man a reason. Fear terrorizes; faith stabilizes. Fear excites the human nature, but faith calms man better than any medicinal tranquilizer. Fear brings sickness; faith brings health. Fear causes insanity, while faith gives man a sound mind. There just is no common ground on which fear and faith can rest, unless it is the "fear of the Lord."

Fear is contrary to the pattern set for the Christian life. It is difficult to count how many "fear nots" are listed in the Bible, but writers have declared for years that there are 365 of them—one for each day of the year.

At the Shoreditch Tabernacle in England, on March 9, 1880, Charles Spurgeon introduced his sermon by saying, " 'Fear not' is a plant which grows very plentifully in God's garden. If you look through the lily beds of Scripture you will continually find by the side of other flowers the sweet 'fear nots' peering out from among doctrines and precepts, even as violets look up from their hiding places of green leaves."

God is neither pleased nor served when we fear the majesty of the person of Jesus Christ in a terrorized manner. It is very common for the devil to interrupt our devotion with a challenge to our worthiness to love and be loved by so majestic a being as God Himself, until we find ourselves asking, "How dare I think that He is my Beloved, and that I am His." But when John the Beloved, on the Isle of Patmos, fell at the feet of Jesus in terror, he was told to "fear not" (Revelation 1:17). We need to learn the balance of letting the Lord be glorious to us, but still be near us. We do well to exalt Him upon the throne, but we must remember that we are seated with Him on that throne. When meditating on His perfection, we do well to remember that He has perfection of mercy as well as of holiness. Fear not to love, relate to, and enjoy the Lord. Our safety lies in trusting Jesus and not in being afraid of Him. No soul has been saved or delivered by being afraid of Christ, just as no prodigal will find forgiveness by being afraid of his father.

Faith is despised when we fear in the midst of a desperate situation. There is no such thing as a hopeless case that is entrusted to the care of Jesus. Much of life is beyond our control, but nothing in our puny little lives is ever beyond His capacity. Fearing inflation will not make it subside any more than worrying about recession will turn the economy back to an upswing. It is not fear but faith that can change the events in our lives from poverty to plenty and from failure to success. It is not fear but faith that moves the hand of God on behalf of His troubled children.

When Joshua stood with the Lord on the mountain viewing the Promised Land into which Joshua was commissioned to take the children of Israel, God told Joshua, ". . . Be strong and of a good courage; be not afraid, neither be thou dismayed . . ." (Joshua 1:9). We are not simply commanded to give no place to fear, but we are exhorted to make much room for courage, for courage is a holding pattern for faith. Courage, God's positive replacement for the negative of fear, is a source of strength for all believers. "Be of good courage, and he shall strengthen your heart, all ye that hope in the Lord" (Psalms 31:24). Courage enables us to endure reverses and suffering, for following Christ is not without its difficulties. There is a moral conflict, a spiritual warfare, a "striving against sin" that demands courage in the believer.

16
Faith Versus Unbelief

When Thomas Paine wrote, "These are the times that try men's souls," he may well have been talking about this particular weekend, for the events these eleven men had been through were both mind boggling and emotionally exhausting. It had started with a pleasant observing of the Passover feast in an upper room, but the pleasantries began to diminish at the announcement of a traitor's presence, and even the magnificent teaching that followed the fellowship meal was overridden by the events in the garden.

The smoking torches, the menacing clanging of Roman armor, coupled with the clandestine arrest of their leader reduced the courage of these men to crass cowardice, and ten of them fled hastily into the darkness of the night, eventually regrouping back in the upper room. One stayed with the arrested one, and another followed from afar.

Jerusalem was soon filled with the drama of the trial, mockery, scourging, and ultimate Crucifixion, and the eyewitness account of the tragedy as told by Peter and John overwhelmed the eleven with grief and despair.

The morning's events had seemed to compound their hopelessness, for Mary Magdalene had reported to them that the body of Jesus was gone, and in its place were two angels sitting on the burial slab proclaiming that Jesus had risen from the dead; but when Peter and John went to check it out, all they could see were folded grave clothes in the empty tomb.

What trickery did the priests of Israel have in mind in se-
creting Christ's body away? Or could it be that the Romans
were behind this charade to discredit the priesthood? In
either case, why were both sides blaming the disciples for the
disappearance of the crucified body?

It was at this point that Christ "appeared unto the eleven
as they sat at meat, and *upbraided them with their unbelief* and
hardness of heart, because they believed not them which had
seen him after he was risen" (Mark 16:14, italics added).

Never had these men received a tongue-lashing that
equaled this one. At first it was hard to believe that this was
the same loving, gentle, compassionate Jesus with whom
they had lived and ministered for nearly three years. His eyes
fairly flashed with indignation as He scolded them for their
"incredulity and obstinancy" (Mark 16:14 JERUSALEM).

It would seem that what the eleven needed most was comfort and consolation, but what they got was criticism and
censure. Why? Had the cross hardened Jesus? Was He overwhelmed with disappointment in the behavior of these men?
Or was he seeking to correct a fatal flaw in them?

Far better than they, Jesus knew the extreme danger of
their unbelief and faithlessness. Without faith it would be
impossible for them to please God (*see* Hebrews 11:6). Their
salvation, sanctification, justification, and righteousness
could come only by faith. Their spiritual walk, talk, standing, and work must be by faith. In spite of all that Christ had
taught and imparted unto them, they couldn't even stay
alive spiritually without faith. Faith is fundamental to the
spiritual realm. It is the bottom line, the prime ingredient,
the unparalleled force in Christian living. It is the absolute
irreducible minimum without which we will continue to be
locked up in our tiny time-space dimension, totally unaware
of and unable to contact a timeless and limitless God.

Jesus was merely giving His disciples a rapid review in fundamentals, for He knew not only the dangers of their unbelief; He knew also the total needlessness of it, for He had given them all the availability to faith they could ever need. He had opened the Old Testament Scriptures to them even as recently as on the road to Emmaus after His Resurrection. Previous to this He had spent nearly three years teaching them verbally while didactically demonstrating the reality of the kingdom of God and the veracity of the Word of God. In this matter of their incredulity He had clearly told them of His impending death and subsequent Resurrection on at least seven occasions, becoming more and more specific each time.

Furthermore, these eleven had the eyewitness testimony of the two Marys, the two disciples who had entered the empty tomb, plus the two disciples who had walked and talked with Jesus on the road to Emmaus. Why three testimonies of two witnesses each? It was so that "in the mouth of two or three witnesses every word may be established" (Matthew 18:16).

Their unbelief was not a lack of availability of faith, but was fundamentally a refusal to allow that faith to function. As the Living Bible puts it, they were reproached by Christ Jesus for "their stubborn refusal to believe" (Mark 16:14). They were so agitated with their own fears that they wouldn't appropriate the faith that had previously been stored in them. Instead of responding out of their abundant supply, they reacted negatively to their abstruse situation. They responded to their soulish senses rather than to the sacred Scriptures, thereby allowing themselves to be immobilized by fear in place of being energized by their faith. They chose unbelief by action and attitude, and Jesus intervened quite drastically to reverse their choice; and He still does with us!

Faith, in one measure or another, abounds everywhere, for "... God hath dealt to every man the measure of faith" (Romans 12:3). Even the secular world is dependent upon it. Our monetary system, our credit cards, our checking accounts, and our savings deposits are all predicated upon faith. Faith is evidenced every time we fly in a plane piloted by someone we have not even met. We're exercising faith when we eat in a restaurant or drive in traffic, and certainly our willingness to ride the roller coaster evidences faith of some sort.

The problem of saint and sinner alike is not that they have no faith, but that they are very selective as to the object of their faith. While exercising great faith in an untried political candidate, they often deny having any faith toward God. In spite of their implicit faith in a mail-order catalog, they repulse any faith in the Bible. They have sufficient faith in the scientists to go to the moon, but not enough faith in God to go to church.

Still, in spite of their repeated disclaimings of faith in God, the Bible says that they are without excuse, for they have been given a measure of faith. Furthermore, "The heavens declare the glory of God; and the firmament sheweth his handywork. Day unto day uttereth speech, and night unto night sheweth knowledge. There is no speech nor language, where their voice is not heard" (Psalms 19:1–3), David declared.

Paul wrote similarly in saying, "Because that which may be known of God is manifest in them; for God hath shewed it unto them. For the invisible things of him from the creation of the world are clearly seen, being understood by the things that are made, even his eternal power and Godhead; so that they are without excuse" (Romans 1:19, 20). God has revealed enough of Himself in nature above and around us to trigger our faith into action. We all have a starting point for faith. Even the "big bang" theory of creation brings men face to face with a beginning and a beginner.

No, men are not without faith in God; they are willfully functioning in unbelief in spite of the manifest proofs around them, very much as the disciples did after the Crucifixion of Christ. They will not believe the evidences presented daily, nor will they accept the testimony of those who have been participants in God's goodness. Whether through fear, wonder, or rebellion, the carnal nature of man grasps unbelief as though it were a lifeline to a sinking swimmer, when, in fact, it is a confirmed one-way ticket into hell itself, for Jesus declared, ". . . if ye believe not that I am he, ye shall die in your sins" (John 8:24), and ". . . he that believeth not shall be damned" (Mark 16:16). None are doomed for lack of faith, but rather for an unwillingness to exercise that faith toward Christ.

Unbelief is the mother sin; from it issue all others. When speaking of the work of the Holy Spirit in the world, Jesus told His disciples, "When he is come, he will reprove the world of sin . . . because they believe not on me" (John 16:8, 9). All of the iniquity for which men and women manifest a propensity stems from this fundamental sin of unbelief—the unwillingness to let the faith that God has imparted and inspired be released back to God—for where unbelief is preeminent, evil will predominate. "Take heed, brethren, lest there be in any of you an evil heart of unbelief, in departing from the living God" (Hebrews 3:12).

Unbelief is not the opposite of faith; it is the absence of faith. (Fear is faith's opposite.) Where unbelief prevails, faith's efficacy is stifled and faith's operation is opposed. Even Jesus "did not many mighty works there because of their unbelief " (Matthew 13:58). When Jesus went to his

home territory, "He marvelled because of their unbelief . . ."
and "He could there do no mighty work . . ." (Mark 6:6, 5).
If the Son of God was prevented from releasing divine power
in the presence of overwhelming unbelief, it should not
amaze us that mere men are seriously impeded in their work
for God in today's unbelieving society. For unbelief short-
circuits the flow of faith, grounding it much as a metal kite
string grounds an electrical transmission line.

Little wonder, then, that the desperate father of the de-
monized son cried, ". . . Lord, I believe; help thou mine unbelief" (Mark 9:24). He wanted nothing within him that
could restrict the flow of God's delivering power. The need
was too desperate for him to hide in his belief. He wanted a
genuine, working faith that was completely unhampered by
unbelief. He not only got it, but he also got the results he desired—his boy was delivered.

Was Jesus too hard on His disciples in upbraiding them
for their unbelief? No, a thousand times no! He knew the
end result of that unbelief would so deteriorate the faith He
had imparted unto them that they would eventually abandon themselves.

Courage is drawn from the Scriptures. To neglect the
Bible is to prepare the way for fear and trembling. Courage
needs an illuminated path, and the Bible is "a lamp unto
[our] feet, and a light unto [our] path" (Psalms 119:105).
Courage also needs confidence of being right and requires
hope, and God's Word is our assurance of right and our
source of hope.

God never tells us to fear not and be courageous without
helping us to be strong and courageous. To Joshua the
climactic word was ". . . for the Lord thy God is with thee
whithersoever thou goest" (Joshua 1:9). How can we be
afraid when the Lord is with us? How can terror smite us in

our inner hearts when Christ is enthroned on those very hearts?

Obviously fear should be handled as quickly as possible, for the longer we wait the stronger it gets. Fear of the enemy can quickly become unbelief in the protection of God. Fear of failure easily becomes unbelief in God's presence and power, whereas fear of present problems already borders on unbelief in God's provision and promises.

Either we handle our fear, or our fear will soon handle us. If we give in to cowardice, we will forever forfeit courage. If we live in dread, we will soon be filled with doubt, and this is a luxury no Christian can afford to maintain. If you don't believe me, ask the disciples.

17

Faith Versus Doubt

Poor Peter! He was such an energetic enthusiast that his mouth continually got him into trouble and earned him several nicknames, such as "the rock," "son of thunder," and "little faith." This last title was appended to him by Jesus when Peter's walking on the water became such a failure that he had to cry to Jesus to save him. "And immediately Jesus stretched forth his hand, and caught him, and said unto him, O thou of little faith, wherefore didst thou doubt?" (Matthew 14:31). "Little faith" comes from the compound *oligó pistos* in the Greek and is a word found virtually nowhere except in the synoptic Gospels. It does not signify the total absence of faith but refers to a great diminishing of that faith. The more Peter looked at the pressing problem, the smaller his faith became. He was set on an unbelieving course that offered him nothing but disaster.

The Greek word Jesus used for "doubt" is *distazō*, which fundamentally means "to waver (in opinion), or to doubt." At the incident of the withered fig tree "Jesus answered and said unto them, Verily I say unto you, If ye have faith, and doubt not, ye shall not only do this which is done to the fig tree, but also if ye shall say unto this mountain, Be thou removed, and be thou cast into the sea; it shall be done" (Matthew 21:21). Here Jesus used a different Greek word for "doubt," *diakrinō*, which means "to withdraw from, to discriminate, hesitate: hence, to doubt, judge, stagger, or waver." This is the same word Paul used when he wrote,

"And he that doubteth is damned if he eat, because he eateth not of faith: for whatsoever is not of faith is sin" (Romans 14:23).

Doubt, as it is used in the New Testament, is a wavering, a hesitancy, or a staggering in faith. It is not unbelief; it is more a poor handling of belief. It is somewhat like trying to tune a weak radio station; it wavers in and out, usually getting less and less discernible until it fades out completely. It is not by accident that Peter was called "weak faith" before Jesus asked him why he doubted. The "stronger station" of the boisterous waves overpowered the signal of faith that was transmitted when Jesus said, "Come."

When we begin to withdraw from God's Word, start to discriminate between what we will read and what we will not, and commence to hesitate in believing what God is saying, we are already involved in doubt. Doubt is uncertain about God's promises; doubt lacks confidence in the God of those promises and considers their fulfillment very unlikely. Doubt puts our experience over against God's Word and trusts our reasoning more than its reality. It is the first tool Satan used against the human race: ". . . Yea, hath God said . . ." (Genesis 3:1), and it is still mightily used against us.

Doubt is not the drawing back of apostasy, which we will discuss later; it is simply hesitating, reexamining, or questioning what has already been proven. It is not honest inquiry; it is a wavering in faith after faith has come. As such, doubt is one of the severest contrarieties to faith, for it dissipates faith after faith has been received. Peter didn't doubt until he had walked on the water for quite a distance. The other disciples, to whom the word of faith was not addressed, were not condemned for doubting; they were totally without faith for water walking.

Doubt is extremely costly for Christians. It prevents what

God has purposed, and often forces the doubter to produce something as a substitute for the faith that had been given. Hezekiah learned this the hard way. When Sennacherib invaded Judah, Hezekiah could not believe in the Lord for deliverance, so he paid over $110 million in gold and at least $1 million in silver (by today's value of gold and silver) in tribute. He had to strip the temple of God to get that much precious metal. Later, when Sennacherib returned in seige against Jerusalem, Hezekiah dared to believe God, and God slew 185,000 Assyrians in one night and delivered Judah without a sword's being lifted or a blow struck. Had he not wavered in his faith the first time he would not have bankrupted his kingdom (*see* 2 Kings 18, 19).

Jacob, also, knew something of the high cost of doubting. Fleeing from the wrath of his brother, Esau, he met God in a dream at Bethel and God promised to be with him during his exile and to return him safely home again. Many years later Jacob headed home with the great increase in family and livestock that God had given him. The angels of God met him, whom Jacob recognized to be God's mighty army (*see* Genesis 32:1, 2). In spite of this and God's assurance of safety, when Jacob heard that Esau was coming out to meet him with 400 men, he feared greatly and sought to appease his brother's wrath by dividing up both his personnel and his livestock, giving each company an appeasement gift for Esau. In all Jacob sent 220 goats, 220 sheep, 30 milk camels, 50 head of cattle, and 30 asses, for a total of 550 head of stock (a fair-sized farm) just because he wavered in his faith in God's promises and protection (*see* Genesis 32:14–18).

Furthermore, we cannot help wondering how much better it would have been for both Moses and Israel if Moses had not doubted God's ability to use his slowness of speech, thereby forcing God to send along his brother Aaron as his spokesman. Moses could have been prophet, priest, and king of Israel just as Jesus later became to His people, but doubt cost Moses the priesthood and eventually produced the golden calf, to say nothing of the other problems Aaron caused him.

Following his great victory on Mount Carmel, Elijah doubted God's protective care when Jezebel sent a message to him threatening his life, and he fled into the desert until he dropped of exhaustion. Except for God's tender mercy he would have died there under the juniper tree (*see* 1 Kings 19).

Abraham and Sarah also paid a high cost for doubting God's promise of a natural son. Ishmael and his descendants have caused Isaac and his descendants perpetual problems ever since. None of this would be in the world today had these two, whom the eleventh chapter of Hebrews calls persons of faith, not dwelt on their circumstances instead of the promise of God.

Doubt is always costly, but it is especially costly when it becomes a dominant force in the moment of crisis. Jacob merely lost cattle, Moses lost a portion of leadership, and Elijah lost some months of ministry hiding in a cave, but doubt can cost us victory in the middle of battle, or even more ironically, doubt can prevent our participation in victory even after the battle has been won. When Israel was under the siege of Ben-hadad there was a desperate famine. Elisha prophesied that within one day there would be a great abundance of food. A lord of the king of Israel openly expressed his doubts, saying that God couldn't even rain enough food from heaven to accomplish His promise, but Elisha simply said, "... Behold, thou shalt see it with thine eyes, but shalt not eat thereof" (2 Kings 7:2). That night God terrorized the Syrians, who fled, abandoning their camp and its provisions. When three lepers discovered this and reported it to the king, this very same lord was appointed to have charge of the gate, and the starving population trampled him under foot in their haste to get to the abundance of food. He saw the victory and the fulfillment of God's promise, but he never tasted of it. His doubt disqualified him from being a participant.

When God speaks, faith flows, and we generally believe and obey. But in the action of obedience our minds begin to rationalize the situation, often producing doubts of such magnitude as to totally short-circuit our faith and make it of no effect. The old cliché is well worth remembering: "Never doubt in the darkness what you trusted in the light." The time for double-checking is when God is speaking. Once we get into the battle, it is too late to try to determine "hath God said." Having put our hands to the plow, it is far too late to look back. If obedience was an act of faith, doubt, which will stop faith's action, will soon produce disobedience, and great will be the penalty thereof.

Are any of us immune to doubts? Once the sweet song of God's communication is replaced with the croaking of frogs in the blackness of night, don't all of our hearts begin to skip a beat in hesitancy? The key to dispelling doubt seems to be a consistent review of what produced the faith within us in the first place. Revive the relationship; review the promise; renew the commitment, and doubt can gain no foothold.

Conversely, resurveying the problem, speaking our fears afresh, and introspectively searching our hearts for the resources necessary to produce victory will become a breeding ground for doubt. Since doubt is too costly a luxury to be allowed in any Christian life, we must learn to take decisive action against its entrance to our minds, for the longer it remains the more difficult it will be to displace it.

One of the fatal characteristics of doubt is that it presumes that what we see, hear, feel, and taste in this world is the real, and what God speaks of in His spiritual kingdom is unreal. But if God says it is real, not only is it real, but by faith we can reach into His realm and make it become a living reality in our world of sense and space.

How we need to be on guard against presumption, for we lack enough facts in the case to presume the solution! We do far better to stay with "thus saith the Lord" than to presume we know what He wants to say, has said, or is about to say; but that is the subject of our next chapter.

18

Faith Versus Presumption

A flying instructor in Alaska presumed that it was a thin cloud ahead of him, so in his haste he flew into it rather than around it. Unfortunately for him, the cloud had formed around a mountain peak, and it took a team of expert mountain climbers several days to recover his body for burial. I can't help but rejoice that we were flying by precision, not presumption, the day he gave me my first flying lesson in a float plane.

In California a man attended a Christian banquet where he heard that he should prosper as his soul prospers (*see* 3 John 2). Numerous testimonies of success stories involving businessmen who had been saved inspired this man to "trust God" in a business venture of his own. He mortgaged his house, sold his new car, quit his job, where he had both seniority and security, and went into business, presuming that God would make it prosper, as others had declared He would. The venture was doomed from the beginning, plunging the man into bankruptcy.

In the East a young mother had just given her preschool daughter her insulin shot and sat in front of the television holding the tot tightly in her arms. Both mother and daughter had developed a near trauma over these repeated shots, so it was time for mutual comfort. On that day's Christian telecast the interviewed guest told of having received a dramatic healing from diabetes and had never taken an injection of insulin from that day until the moment of the broadcast. Desire sprang up in this young mother's heart, and in an emotional outburst she said, "Darling, you'll never feel an injection needle again. God is going to heal you, too."

Presuming this hopeful exuberance to be faith, the mother threw all of the insulin and injection paraphernalia into the garbage can, declaring almost in a rote or chant, "God is going to heal my daughter." Unfortunately, the daughter later lapsed into a coma, and but for immediate and expert medical help she would have died.

What went wrong in these cases? Each presumed and discovered that presumption can never substitute for faith nor produce faith. The pilot had ignored his maps and had trusted his instincts; the man ignored his true capabilities and calling, presuming that if others could succeed in business so could he, so he trusted the testimony of others; and the mother of the diabetic girl ignored the reality and seriousness of her daughter's illness, presuming that what God had done in another He would automatically do in her daughter, so she trusted her deep desires. None of them had divine faith, but each moved presumptuously into a set of circumstances that produced tragedy, for presumption has a great reputation for tragic endings.

True faith, divine faith, knows; it does not presume! Faith is a settled persuasion, not a pretense or presumption. God's faith comes as the result of a *rhema*, a directed word from the Lord, and flows into the persuasion that "God has said. . . ." It will not go beyond that word, but it does stake its life on that word.

Presumption, on the other hand, lacks a word from the Lord. It assumes that because a promise is written in the Bible it is available to anyone who chooses to act upon it. Interestingly enough, however, none but Naaman has ever been cleansed from leprosy by dipping seven times in the

Jordan River (*see* 2 Kings 5), nor have I ever read of anyone but Peter walking on the Sea of Galilee with Jesus (*see* Matthew 14). These were direct words from God to specific individuals that became faith-producing words. Trying to force God to repeat these miracles by stubbornly stepping over the stern of a ship or by dauntlessly dipping seven times in the Jordan River would not be faith; it would be preposterous presumption. In either case one would get wet, but that is all.

If getting wet were the total penalty for substituting presumption for faith, then it could be viewed as innocuous and even mildly amusing, but presumption is viewed as a very deadly sin in the Word of God.

Of the ten times the word is used in the Bible, six of those are in the Pentateuch, where God was regulating the lives of His newly formed family by laws and ordinances. Its first usage concerned Israel's actions one toward another, "But if a man come *presumptuously* upon his neighbour, to slay him with guile; thou shalt take him from mine altar, that he may die" (Exodus 21:14, italics added), and "But the soul that doeth ought *presumptuously* . . . that soul shall be cut off from among his people" (Numbers 15:30, italics added), and both regulations provide extreme penalties for acting insolently, proudly, or presumptuously, as this Hebrew word implies.

The next time the word is used it is coupled with obedience. After Israel refused to enter the Promised Land because of their fear of giants in the land, God condemned them to a slow, wandering death. Hearing this changed their minds, and they presented themselves to Moses ready for battle, but Moses told them that it was too late, and that God would not go in with them now. "But they *presumed* to go up unto the hill top . . ." (Numbers 14:44, italics added), and the Amalekites and the Canaanites smote them mercilessly. The Hebrew word translated here as "presumed" is *'aphal,* meaning "to swell, be elated, or lifted up."

When this same story is repeated to the second generation, the Hebrew word used in Deuteronomy 1:43 is *ziyd,* meaning "to seethe, to be insolent; be proud, or deal proudly." Israel's disobedience was rooted in elation, insolence, and pride; death was the result.

Twice presumption is linked with the prophetic office. "But the prophet, which shall *presume* to speak a word in my name, which I have not commanded him to speak . . . even that prophet shall die" (Deuteronomy 18:20, italics added), and, two verses later, "When a prophet speaketh in the name of the Lord, if the thing follow not, nor come to pass, that is the thing which the Lord hath not spoken, but the prophet hath spoken it *presumptuously:* thou shalt not be afraid of him" (Deuteronomy 18:22, italics added). Both times the root words mean "to be insolent, arrogant, or presumptuous. The person who pretends or presumes to speak on God's behalf is considered arrogant and proud whether he fakes a message or a faith. The penalty was death.

The one New Testament usage of this word is in the writings of Peter. "But chiefly them that walk after the flesh in the lust of uncleanness, and depise government. *Presumptuous* are they, selfwilled, they are not afraid to speak evil of dignities" (2 Peter 2:10, italics added). The Greek word Peter employs for "presumptuous" is *tolmetes* which means "a daring (audacious) man; presumptuous," and is translated "headstrong" by Goodspeed, and "audacious" in the Twentieth Century New Testament.

In every instance the word *presumptuous* is shown to be a bad character trait that is contrary to the life of a believer who has learned to walk in the Spirit. The presumptuous person is revealed to be insolent, proud, arrogant, and elated or lifted up. He speaks whether God has spoken or not. He acts irrespective of the commands of God, and he predetermines his actions in spite of those commands. Peter says that presumptuous ones "despise government," and they are so self-willed that "they are not afraid to speak evil of dignities" (2 Peter 2:10), even claiming that God spoke to them when, in fact, God did not speak to them at all.

But, of course, none of us would act presumptuously; or would we? I have been in services where spiritual elation and expectation were fanned to such a flame that the entire congregation began to declare their emotions and fervent desires as a word from the Lord to them. They acted presumptuously.

Furthermore, I have seen Christian leaders, whose strength of ministry is in the area of faith, be under such pressure to produce a miracle that they have declared that God had told them things that never came to pass, and have proclaimed dramatic healings that never materialized. They spoke presumptuously.

The desire to make God "look good," or the proud attitude that must have what it wants when it wants it sets the stage for acting presumptuously. Presumptuous persons refuse to allow God to be sovereign and seek to impose their will and way upon the Almighty. They seek to originate faith by their mental attitudes and emotional responses and declare that the product of these inner forces—which at its highest level is natural or human faith—is divine faith. That it is nonproducing doesn't deter the presumptuous person, for pride and arrogance have blinded him to his reversed role with God. He doesn't recognize that he is trying to produce what can only originate in God.

Although few Christians consciously "play God," it is still very possible to act in a presumptuous manner. To discontinue use of prescribed medication just because we have been prayed for is far more presumption than faith. If faith had functioned, healing would have come and medication would be unnecessary. But if we are trying to demonstrate our faith by flushing our prescriptions down the toilet, all in the name of God, we do not hasten our healing; we bring discredit to the work of God. How the press likes to play up such "failures of faith," which are actually only acts of presumption!

Similarly, it is presumption, not faith, when we attempt to speak into existence the things we desire or need. Unless God speaks, nothing will happen, for "mountain-moving faith" must originate in Almighty God, not in presumptuous little men. We are not creators—He is. It is arrogant to try to take His place.

It is presumption rather than faith when we indiscriminately purchase what we want "believing" that God will make the payments for us. God underwrites every program He writes, but He is not responsible for debts incurred by us, aside from His commands.

Some years ago a member of our congregation came into my office to inform me that God had provided a way out of her family's indebtedness and that she had written checks to cover all their bills. This sounded like a victorious miracle in their lives, for we had been counseling them on money management, and I knew the extent of their liabilities.

"How did God provide such a large sum of money?" I asked.

"He hasn't, yet," she said, "but I'm acting in faith by mailing these checks to the creditors. God will have to produce the money before the checks are presented for payment."

I had to point out that what she was about to do was illegal and could, in that state, result in a penitentiary term.

Asking for the envelopes, I threw them into the wastepaper basket, all the while assuring her that if God had spoken, the funds would come and then she could safely write checks against them. The fact that no supernatural miracle produced this vast sum of money proved that she was acting in presumption and not in faith.

There is a very fine line between acting in divine faith and acting in human presumption. In writing the biography of Charles Spurgeon, Russell H. Conwell pointed out how positively Mr. Spurgeon acted when he had heard from God, sometimes even in the face of contrary circumstances. He then admitted that anyone else who sought to follow Mr. Spurgeon's example soon discovered they were functioning in presumption, not in faith. God's methods and message to one person cannot be embraced wholesale by others and made to work. Only God's faith functions in the divine realms, and that faith is communicated by a *rhema,* not by our observations and adaptations.

As surely as no husband has the right to "presume" he knows what his wife is thinking, and no wife is entitled to "presume" she knows her husband's desires and will, so we have no right to "presume" God desires to do, say, or act in any specific way. He's alive; ask Him! He's a person; don't violate Him. He's Almighty God; don't dethrone Him. To do so is to be perilously presumptive, and God not only hates presumption, but He classifies it as a dangerous sin which, under the old covenant, deserved death.

Little wonder, then, that David prayed, "Keep back thy servant also from presumptuous sins; let them not have dominion over me: then shall I be upright, and I shall be innocent from the great transgression" (Psalms 19:13).

Presumption is a great enemy of faith that can never be a substitute for faith. The sin of presumption is forgivable, but since it so often masquerades as faith, it is seldom confessed as a sin. At every emergence of presumption in others let us pray David's prayer, "Keep back thy servant also from presumptuous sins," for unless God helps us we are all subject to mistaking proud arrogance for powerful faith. We must learn to discern between God's faith and our feelings, or presumption will prevail over faith; death, not life, will result; and we will find ourselves trapped in feigned faith that is far more dependent upon feelings than the facts of God's Word.

19

Faith Versus Feeling

When God created His most exalted order of creatures—man—He gave him a highly sensitized emotional nature which could receive stimuli from a variety of sources and translate them into feelings ranging from elation to depression, or from love to hate. Man is a very feeling-oriented creature, and much of his time and energy is spent in producing positive and pleasant feelings.

Because of the amazing complexity of man he may be stimulated pleasantly by a surprising number of different factors. Physical touch can become most pleasurable, as can sound and taste. Pictures of lovers holding hands across a restaurant table while an orchestra plays in the background almost always speak to us of extreme pleasure. Sight is also a strong stimulus for pleasant sensations as illustrated by a person watching a sunset, and even our sense of smell is capable of creating pleasurable responses, as every perfume manufacturer well knows.

Beyond his five senses man can create strong sensations with drugs, food, drink, and sex, but it is in the area of his thought patterns that man seems to stand supremely superior to the animal creation, for man is capable of stirring great inner emotions with nothing more than mental activity. Memories can bring a return of very pleasurable sensations, and hopes visualized as daydreams can stir equally pleasant feelings.

These sensations whose origins are in the soul (the mental

and emotional nature of persons) are the longest-lasting and the most severe of all feelings. Here love, hate, lust, desire, yearnings, and a great host of other feelings have their origins and expressions, often controlling all actions of the body and setting the tenor of the will. These soulish sensations are stimulated as much by word and thought patterns as they are by the five senses, and frequently the person who is enjoying a fervent emotional experience is unaware of just what factor or factors have triggered it.

All persons have but one set of emotions that respond to the divine world, the human world, and the demonic world. A person may be happy because of pleasant earthly situations, because of divine intervention in his life, or because there has been a release from demonic activity, but the emotion, which is only a response, will be the same. The stimulus may differ but the response is similar.

Because of this it is never trustworthy to take guidance solely from our feelings. The coming of God's Word to us in the form of a *rhema* may trigger a very pleasant, peaceful feeling, but we dare not interpret all such feelings as indication that God is speaking to us. The feeling is an effect, not a cause. Whenever we try to produce a cause by stimulating an effect, we will end in fruitless frustration or feigned faith. What we feel is not faith, but when God's faith is flowing through our spirit it may very well induce intense feelings in our soul. We do ourselves a great favor when we learn that our reactions are only emotional responses that add nothing whatever to the working of divine faith.

Some years ago I was conducting special services for a pastor with whom I had taught in a Bible school for several years. His wife was critically ill with cancer. I had worked with this dear saint in the music department of that Bible school and yearned greatly to see God heal her. As the ser-

vices progressed through the week, my prayers for her healing produced greater and greater fervency and expectancy in
me until I had her carried into the church so everyone could
join me in a final time of prayer for her healing before I returned to my own congregation. The sense of God's presence
became so very real that I emotionally announced that she
was healed at that very instant, and that she would show
great signs of that healing the following week. So strong were
my feelings that I told her husband, the pastor, that even if
she died I would recommend against buying a casket too
hastily, for God would raise her from the dead.

The congregation entered into my elated feelings of great
victory and the concluding service ended in great expectation. Unfortunately the facts later proved that I was moving
in feelings, not faith, for one week later, to the very day, they
buried her. Although it greatly shook me, it took their
daughter more than ten years to forgive me for my false pro-
jections. Before and since that incident I have been a channel for God to perform some mighty works of healing, but
I've never had a higher emotional expectancy than I had at
that time. My failure was in misinterpreting my intense feelings as divine faith. God had neither spoken nor released a
divine energy. My love, concern, and pity, had risen to a
fever pitch, but they were not capable of producing faith.

At the opposite end of the spectrum, very recently a pastor
unexpectedly called upon me to anoint and pray for the
healing of one of his parishioners. I had not preached that
morning; I didn't have any sense of emotional or spiritual
flow, and I was physically exhausted, but I heard an inner
voice say, "I want to use you."

When the woman began walking down the aisle toward
me, my heart sank. She was bent, twisted, and walking almost sideways. This called for miracle faith, and I was un-

aware of any faith whatever. Obediently I anointed her with oil and I heard myself pray, "Lord, You know that I'm too tired to feel anything. I am unaware of any faith whatsoever, but please have compassion on ..." at which point my prayer was interrupted by a cracking noise followed by sweet praises. Opening my eyes I was startled to see this little woman completely straightened up, waving her hands with head erect, and praising God. Before I could say a word she began to dance up and down the center aisle of that church, rejoicing in a marvelous display of God's power. Bowing my head I confessed to the Lord that I had not had an ounce of faith, when the Spirit of God spoke within me saying, "That's all right, Judson; I had more than enough."

Although God's great faith had flowed out to this sister, healing her instantly, through the whole experience my only feeling had been amazement that anything had happened at all. God's faith had flowed without stirring any emotion within me, for, "Faith cometh by hearing ..." not by feeling (*see* Romans 10:17).

If, then, the presence of deep feeling does not necessarily signify a flow of divine faith, and the absence of emotional stimuli does not automatically indicate an absence of divine faith, what part do our emotions play in our relating to God? What place is there for feelings?

When Paul stood on Mars Hill in the middle of Athens, he preached about THE UNKNOWN GOD, declaring Him to be the creator of all things including all men: "That they should seek the Lord, if haply they might *feel after him,* and find him, though he be not far from every one of us" (Acts 17:27, italics added). Our emotions are tools that enable us to reach beyond ourselves in our search after God. Religious feelings are often merely manifestations of our deep inner hunger after God Himself. Our conscious, or even subconscious, sense of need inspires an outreach after God in expressions of love, joy, praise, and adoration. These are our feelers as we reach after God much as a plant reaches for a stake or string to climb on.

Furthermore, our feelings often open the gates of our lives to let the King of Glory come in. Our will is seldom motivated without the persuasive power of emotional activity both naturally and spiritually. Just as it requires the power of love to motivate individuals into the lifetime commitment of marriage, so a love flow opens the Christian to a commitment to Christ.

Similarly, our feelings are responses to God's presence in our individual lives or our corporate worship. I would wonder at the person who could stand unmoved in the presence of Jesus, for throughout the Gospels, people were regularly moved by His presence—whether positively or negatively. His acts induce praise; His person inspires worship; and His realized presence stirs a great variety of emotional feelings in our lives.

But whether our feelings are reaching after God, searching to find Him, are opening our soul and spirit to receive Him, or even are responding in ecstasy to His exciting presence, these feelings are not faith, cannot be translated into faith, and can never substitute for faith.

Faith is the force; feeling is but a reaction to that force. Faith is an energy, while feeling is but an excitement caused by that energy. But that same feeling or excitement may be produced by a stimulus other than faith, and that is where the confusion sets in.

The presence of great faith may inspire a great feeling of wonder and awe, but I felt these emotions the first time I stood on the rim of the Grand Canyon in Arizona. The flow of divine faith may produce a near-rapturous feeling of love, but I enjoyed this emotion while watching my bride come down the aisle toward me many years ago. Faith functioning may engender a tremendous sense of expectancy, but I felt this every time I paced the hospital room waiting for the birth of one of my children.

It is obvious, then, that the emotion is not the evidence; it is but the effect. If faith triggers the emotion, then the feeling may be a part of the expression of faith, but if something other than faith has triggered the emotion, no matter how strongly we may feel and express that emotion, it can produce nothing more than an equal emotional response in others. It is powerless to substitute for faith.

Because all of us have tasted the bitter deception of misinterpreting our feelings as faith, we may honestly question whether feelings are a friend or a foe to faith. Do they aid or arrest faith's operation?

As tools that enable us to reach out to God, our feelings, (we must admit), are a true friend of faith. Without those deep longings, yearnings, and cryings in our soul, it is unlikely that our spirit would push its way into God at any time. When our emotions help to open us to God's presence, they are obviously a friend of faith. Love, joy, and peace cause us to sing, "Holy Spirit, thou art welcome in this place." Furthermore, when our emotions assist us in expressing our faith, our feelings are a friend of faith.

However, if we allow our feelings to become the evidence of faith's presence, those feelings have become a foe to faith. If we set our emotional senses as the standard by which we measure faith, those feelings are automatic foes of our faith. If, God forbid, we should try to substitute our feelings for God's faith, we will quickly discover that those feelings are a dangerous foe that will completely arrest the action of true faith.

Hence it is not the feeling that becomes a friend or foe to faith; it is how we channel that feeling. It can assist in attaining faith, or it can resist in releasing faith.

While none of us wants a religion without feelings, having learned the old cliché, "If you take emotion out of religion, you'll have no motion at all," still each of us wisely fears any religion that depends heavily upon emotional fervor to perpetuate its faith, or even worse, to produce that faith. The divine order seems to be: faith, fact, feeling. That is, we believe God's Word; situations change, and we respond emotionally to that change. Any attempt to move from emotion to faith is a reversal of God's order and is doomed to failure since our feelings are no more capable of producing divine faith than our intellect is. A feeling-oriented faith is as much feigned faith as a mere intellectual faith is feigned faith.

20

Faith Versus Intellect

The Holy Spirit told the Hebrews, "Now faith is the substance of things hoped for, the evidence of things not seen" (Hebrews 11:1), indicating that faith deals with the unknown, the unseen, and the unpredictable. Faith is the channel that enables God and man to communicate and is the bridge between their differing realms. Faith enables a person living in our time-space dimension to reach into God's limitless eternity and apprehend spiritual realities, bringing them back into the experience of our carnal world.

As such, faith is a force functioning beyond natural wisdom, for, as Paul declared, ". . . in the wisdom of God the world by wisdom knew not God . . ." (1 Corinthians 1:21). The knowledge of God is not a by-product of a university education, nor is it obtainable merely through a systematic and concerted study of religion or the Bible. Even the seminary graduate with his conferred degree in religion or divinity does not have a knowledge of God and His world as the result of his education. True knowledge of God comes as revelation, not as rote learning.

> But as it is written, Eye hath not seen, nor ear heard, neither have entered into the heart of man, the things which God hath prepared for them that love him. But God hath revealed them unto us by his Spirit: for the Spirit searcheth all things, yea, the deep things of God.
>
> 1 Corinthians 2:9, 10

When the human mind attempts to comprehend the divine world and all of its availabilities to us, it just fails to compute; instead it gives us a readout saying "reject." God knew this from the beginning for He told us, ". . . the natural man receiveth not the things of the Spirit of God: for they are foolishness unto him; neither can he know them, because they are spiritually discerned" (1 Corinthians 2:14). As surely as my knowledge of the workings of an organ and my ability to play it cannot qualify me to understand and operate a 747 jet liner, even so, knowledge about worldly things cannot qualify or greatly aid us in comprehending or apprehending spiritual realities. Faith, and only faith, is the channel for spiritual revelation. That faith must be founded in, focused on, and fused with God Himself or it will be impotent and ineffective. Paul said that his preaching was ". . . in demonstration of the Spirit and of power: That your faith should not stand in the wisdom of men, but in the power of God" (1 Corinthians 2:4, 5).

If faith could be produced by human intellect, then our wisest persons would have the most faith, while the poorly educated would have the least. Since both the Word of God and human experience teach that this is not so, we must guard against misinterpreting knowledge as faith. In my book *Let Us Abide* I call the faith that is produced by memorizing and quoting verses of Scripture on a given subject "paper faith." By exercising our intellect upon and in the Word of God, we may generate a small level of believing, but it is only "paper faith." No revelation has come, no divine communication has been heard; we've merely researched the subject, learned the promises, and declared that we believe. Nothing of spiritual value will come of such productions. Our intellect is incapable of producing divine energy, for it is inexorably tuned to the earthlies and cannot reach, unaided, into the spirituals.

How often we have tried to produce faith by sharing testimonies, but though the faith experience of another may be inspirational, illuminating, and informative, it cannot produce faith. Occasionally, of course, God releases faith to us as we are listening to a testimony, but the testimony is not causal; it is incidental. The testimony may have informed the intellect and inspired the emotions, but only God can create faith in the human spirit.

Faith will not be produced by any action of our intellect, even the reading of this book, for far from producing the faith of God, ". . . the carnal mind is enmity against God . . ." (Romans 8:7). My natural reasoning reacts against God rather than responds to God. The undisciplined mind says that there is no God, no heaven, no life after death, and no availability of spiritual realities in the here and now. It is only in the spirit of man that such awareness can take root, grow, and blossom like fragrant roses. Faith flows from the Spirit of God into the spirit of man, and then man's quickened spirit disciplines his intellect to respond in accordance with faith's illumination. At this point the intellect becomes a partner with faith in directing the responses of the individual in accordance with this imparted faith.

Just as all extremes are dangerous, it is improper and unscriptural to totally divorce the action of our intellect from the faith in our spirit, for although our intellect cannot cause faith, it can, and should, channel faith's action. It is neither glorifying to God nor beneficial to men for people to act irrationally and unreasonably because they have received a flow of faith. Paul wrote, "My brothers, don't be like excitable children but use your intelligence! By all means be innocent as babes as far as evil is concerned, but where your minds are concerned be full-grown men" (1 Corinthians 14:20 PHILLIPS).

If, as Weatherhead wrote, "Faith is the psychological frame of mind in which God can get near enough to man in order to do His work," then intelligent, reasonable action needs to follow the inception of faith so that God's work will be fully accomplished through faith's operation.

God does not impart faith into man's spirit so that man can completely turn his mind off. The function of faith calls for full cooperation and participation by the whole of man. Jesus said, "Thou shalt love the Lord thy God with all thy heart, and with all thy soul, *and with all thy mind,* and with all thy strength: this is the first commandment" (Mark 12:30, italics added). Since "faith . . . worketh by love" (Galatians 5:6), involving the mind in loving automatically involves the mind in the operation of faith.

We are always responsible for our actions in life. Not even a flow of divine faith can divest us of this accountability for our behavior, yet it is distressing to see well-meaning and normally well-balanced individuals behave as though they were unintelligent, and all in the name of faith. Oftentimes all aids to healing are rejected, sound financial policies are abandoned, exaggerative projects are commenced, and luxurious spending sprees are indulged in, all because individuals believe they have faith. Is faith incompatible with rational living? Or is faith the true reason for living rationally?

None in our generation will enter into more faith than Jesus Christ, yet His behavior was intelligent, rational, and normal. He even performed supernatural works so naturally as to confound the bystanders. He never needed to "grandstand" His miracles or build a particular psychological atmosphere in order to work miracles; He just released His faith with a word, a touch, or an act.

Far from proving our faith, abnormal, unbalanced, and thoughtless behavior usually proves the absence of true faith. Where do we read of people leaving the healing presence of Jesus "claiming" their healing? They were either healed, or they were not healed. Had the lame limped away, the blind been led away, and the dead remained buried, no one would have believed that Jesus was the Christ, the Son of God, even if they had all "claimed and proclaimed" their healing.

True faith is productive; there are always results. Divine faith does not call for mindless ignoring of the facts; it changes the facts, for it is the forceful function of faith to give us "the substance of things hoped for" (Hebrews 11:1).

To demand a renunciation of the intellect and to ignore genuine facts as part of the operation of faith hints strongly of cultism. While I recognize that truth and facts may not correlate immediately, inasmuch as truth comes through revelation, and faith and facts are discerned by knowledge, still, truth absolutely must involve facts, for the entire world of the supernatural is as natural to God as breathing is natural to man.

Some argue that spiritual truth is communicated to their spirit and does not involve their mind at all. Still God says, "This is the covenant that I will make with them after those days, saith the Lord, I will put my laws into their hearts, and *in their minds will I write them*" (Hebrews 10:16, italics added). God doesn't entirely bypass our minds; He has graven His principles, purposes, and precepts in them. He anticipates and expects rational responses.

Our intellect need not become a problem to our faith. Actually it can be a protection to it. We get into trouble when we seek to produce faith through intellectual action rather than by fellowship with God, and that calamity is greatly amplified when we refuse to allow our God-given and God-directed intellect to direct, protect, and reflect our faith.

Unfeigned faith is not a leap into the dark; it is a cautious step into new light. It is not blindly doing what "seems to be right" (*see* Proverbs 14:12; 16:25); it is courageously doing what God has shown to be right. Unfeigned faith is not a guess; it is guidance. It is not a hope; it is a happening. It doesn't ignore facts; it changes them.

If the mind must be turned off, it is feigned faith. If we must progressively function contrary to sound reason, it is feigned faith. If we must pretend that things are different when it is obvious even to a casual observer that they are unchanged, then it is feigned faith.

This generation cannot be turned to God by feigned faith; we must contend for unfeigned faith—faith that is so productive that all may observe the results. The Jews were incited by a resurrected, living Lazarus, not by Martha's confession, "I know that he shall rise again in the resurrection at the last day" (John 11:24). Martha's intellectual believing hadn't changed anything the full three days that Lazarus had been buried, but the faith-filled words of Jesus, ". . . Lazarus, come forth" (John 11:43) imparted life to the dead, reunited the sorrowing, and stimulated the Jews to crucify Jesus. When faith functioned, facts changed. The grave clothes were not unwrapped to evidence their faith but to release the bound and now gloriously living Lazarus.

What, then, is the balance between faith versus intellect? The intellect cannot create faith, but it should cooperate with it. Faith may initially reach beyond the intellect, but it will not abandon it. Faith is supremely spiritual, but it need not be irrational.

If, as we shall see in the next chapter, faith and works are inseparable, then the action of our intellect is important to direct the operation of the working of faith.

Faith becomes feigned faith when the intellect substitutes for faith, not when it substantiates that faith, and all feigned faith tends to lean heavily on works, hoping to make up by doing what it lacks in being.

21

Faith Versus Works

When James wrote, ". . . faith without works is dead" (James 2:20), he began a minor controversy that continues to this day, for Paul had already clearly written ". . . that a man is not justified by the works of the law, but by the faith of Jesus Christ . . . for by the works of the law shall no flesh be justified" (Galatians 2:16). Positioning James as an antagonist of Paul has been popular with some people for many years, but, quite frankly, it is a tempest in a teapot.

Faith and works need not be antagonistic one to the other any more than faith and intellect are diametrically opposed. Perhaps if we could see faith and works *compared* and *contrasted,* we could understand that they can either be *competitive* or *completive.*

Perhaps we should first compare and contrast the writings of these two apostles before we try to compare faith and works. J. Gresham Machen, in *What Is Faith?,* says simply, "The difference, then, between Paul and James is a difference of terminology." Paul certainly taught that faith involved works, for he spoke of ". . . faith which worketh by love" (Galatians 5:6), and "Remembering without ceasing your work of faith . . ." (1 Thessalonians 1:3). He did not see faith as an inactive, impassive attitude but as a vital, viable force to be both received and released. On the other hand, James did not see works as efficacious without faith. Dr. James Hastings, in the *Dictionary of the Bible,* says:

When read from his own historical standpoint, James' teachings are free from any disaccord with those of Paul, who as strongly as James denies all value to a faith which does not work by love. In short, James is not depreciating faith: with him, too, it is faith that is reckoned unto righteousness (2:23), though only such a faith as shows itself in works can be so reckoned, because a faith which does not come to fruitage in works is dead, non-existent. He is rather deepening the idea of faith, and insisting that it includes in its very conception something more than an otiose intellectual assent.

James and Paul, both writing under the inspiration of the Holy Spirit, are not in conflict; they complete each other. James speaks of faith that even the devils have—an intellectual assent to the existence and claims of God, while Paul speaks of divine saving faith that is a gift of the grace of God. The level of the faith differs tremendously, hence the action expected of the faith is different. Saving faith cannot be earned by works, while dead, intellectual faith must be expressed by active works. The divine faith is unproducible by works, while the natural faith is unprofitable without works. It is almost as though James says that works are the result of faith, while Paul declares that works cannot result in faith.

So faith and works, when compared and contrasted, can either be competitive or completive, depending on which comes first—the faith or the works. If works seek to become the cause of faith, then they are, obviously, competitive, but if our works seek to communicate our faith they become completive. It is very much like the two oars of a rowboat, one labeled "faith," and the other called "works." Either used without the other will merely turn the boat in circles, but when both oars are used equally, the boat moves forward through the water.

In this present generation it appears that much "faith" teaching leans heavily on human works to produce the faith. Without actually defining their terms some teachers spend much time teaching their constituents what works will produce faith. It seems that they may have confused their prepositions, for they speak more of what works *for* faith than they share about the works *of* faith. Unfortunately, no matter how diligently one may enter into works *for* faith, those works will never produce faith.

Universally, piety is taught as a work that will produce faith. Since Old Testament times, prayers, church attendance, fastings, and religious service have been projected as key acts that will father faith. Paul took a firm stance against the concept that doing the works of the law could generate faith, illustrating his position by faithless Israel, who reveled in scrupulous observance of the sacred oracles. The human spirit is comfortable with a code or rule book, but rites, ceremonies, liturgy, ritual, and service are not faith producing; they are intended to be channels for the expression and enjoyment of faith.

Second only to piety is the emphasis upon contributions as a work *for* faith. The concept of "seed faith" has given a doctrinal solemnity to the concept that if you give God (or God's servant or program) a sacrificial gift, it will result in God's giving "one-hundred fold" back to the donor. The offering is no longer a gift of love; it is an investment with a guaranteed return. The theme of the teaching seems to be that faith is producible and increasable by giving money. If this were so, then the rich would have the maximum amount of faith and the poor would have the least, but Jesus seemed to teach quite the opposite in his story of the widow's mite (*see* Mark

12:42). Although giving of our finances is commanded by God and commended by Christ, the Bible teaches that all giving expresses faith, but that expression cannot engender faith. Faith is not purchasable, nor is it receivable by putting God under obligation to us by our financial contributions to His work.

Another form of works *for* faith is the insistence upon a consistent positive confession. This emphasis teaches that we have whatever our mouth proclaims, so refusing to accept the reality of a negative situation and declaring it to be a positive one will produce sufficient faith as to change the circumstances. Since I've devoted an entire chapter to this theme, may I simply remark that faith is produced when God speaks, not when man speaks. No amount of positive confession can produce faith, but it can release faith in a most wonderful way. If faith were generated by our speaking, the religions that rely heavily upon the chant and rote repetition of religious phrases would evidence great faith. If mere positive profession could produce faith, then our American politicians would be men of great faith, especially in an election year.

Analogous to this is the teaching that one should testify to their healing whether the facts support the testimony or not. It is a matter of "testimony before the fact" in order to produce sufficient faith to produce the fact. This defies the very word *testimony*. If it has not happened and we declare that it has, we are liars; we are not producing faith. The purpose of a testimony is to declare and exhibit the works of God, not to effect faith in the person giving the testimony. Surely the Christian should be as faithful to the truth as a witness in a court of law. It is the facts, not the feelings, that are required in a testimony. Pretense and presumption in a courtroom testimony are considered perjury. The sharing of a testimony is a good "work," but it is not intended to procreate faith, merely proclaim it.

Another work *for* faith that is widely taught is the abandoning of all medical assistance as a process of generating more faith. Medicines are disposed of, doctors are abandoned and often openly criticized, and all prognoses are declared to be false. The consequences have been published on the front pages of our newspapers, especially when they concerned minor children. If the absence of medical assistance was faith producing, then the inhabitants of third-world countries would have the most faith, for medical help is available to very few of them. It does not produce faith in or of God to castigate the medical profession. If one chooses, as an expression of his faith, to bypass their services, that is one thing. But when we seek to create faith by deliberately endangering our health, or the well-being of those for whom we are responsible, in an attempt to create faith by these works, we are deluded.

Performing works *for* faith is getting the cart before the horse. The Scripture speaks of works *of* faith: works which release, express, and proclaim our faith. Paul, remember, says that "faith . . . worketh by love" (Galatians 5:6), and in his beautiful love chapter in 1 Corinthians he defines some of the works of love.

> This love of which I speak is slow to lose patience—it looks for a way of being constructive. It is not possessive: it is neither anxious to impress nor does it cherish inflated ideas of its own importance.
>
> Love has good manners and does not pursue selfish advantage. It is not touchy. It does not keep account of evil or gloat over the wickedness of other people. On the contrary, it shares the joy of those who live by the truth.

Love knows no limit to its endurance, no end to its trust, no fading of its hope; it can outlast anything. Love never fails.

1 Corinthians 13:4–8 PHILLIPS

While Paul speaks of love as the outstanding work *of* faith, James speaks of obedience as being a prime work of faith, and he parades the obedience of Abraham in placing his son Isaac upon the sacrificial altar, and the obedience of Rahab in Jericho (*see* James 2:21–25). Where true divine faith is flowing, both love and obedience will be growing.

Perhaps the major issue is not faith *or* works, or even faith *and* works, but *faith that works,* for Hebrews 11 shows that faith actually works; it produces!

By [faith] the elders obtained a good report (v.2).

By faith Abel . . . obtained witness that he was righteous, God testifying of his gifts . . . (v.4).

By faith Enoch was translated that he should not see death; and was not found, because God has translated him (v.5).

By faith Noah . . . prepared an ark . . . condemned the world . . . became heir of the righteousness which is by faith (v.7).

By faith Abraham . . . obeyed . . . sojourned in the land of promise (vv.8, 9).

Through faith Sarah herself . . . was delivered of a child when she was past age (v.11).

And so it goes throughout the chapter. The faith of these saints worked. Something happened. It was not so much a matter of their proclamation as it was of their production. Their believing affected their behavior; their faith fostered works. They received a divine faith that worked, and the world has been a better place because of it.

One wonders why so much of the declared faith of the twentieth century is so anemic and lifeless. Perhaps we are trying to manufacture faith through our works rather than manifest our faith through our works. Maybe, once again, we have fallen into the trap of reversing the cause-and-effect relationships. Faith is the cause; works are the effect.

Or is our impotency of faith due to the object of our faith? So much emphasis is being placed on "prosperity teaching," which implies that the level of our faith is the only limiting factor in the acquisition of possessions. "If you have faith for a Cadillac, drive a Cadillac," they teach, "but if you only have faith for a Chevrolet, then drive a Chevrolet." Has God actually imparted His divine energy so we can have everything we want? Is the true purpose of faith health, wealth, and happiness, or have we confused the American dream with the divine provision?

22
Faith Versus Prosperity

At the conclusion of my sermon at a Fourth of July rally recently a guest in our country told me, "I thank God that there is at least one preacher who has separated his patriotism from his theology."

"What do you mean?" I asked him. "I'm a true patriot; I love America deeply."

"I can appreciate that," he responded, "but you don't seem to make God and country all one. You don't mix the American dream with the divine provision."

This gave me food for thought that evening. So much of the preaching and teaching at conferences where faith is emphasized seems to present the American dream of "health, wealth, and happiness" as a by-product of being born again.

Simplistically stated, the American philosophy seems to be "love things, and use people to get them," while the philosophy of the Scriptures is "love people, and use things to bless them." When we are rightly related to God's principles, He delights in abundantly giving such things as we can use to bless people. Since "every beast of the forest is mine, and the cattle upon a thousand hills" (Psalms 50:10), it is never difficult for God to lavishly give to His people. Job, Abraham, Jacob, Isaac, David, and Solomon are just a few biblical examples of God's abundant wealth shared with faithful men.

That God is well able to care for His children is incontestable. His care for Israel in the wilderness is abundant proof of this. That God has promised to supply our needs is clearly stated by Paul: "But my God shall supply all your need according to his riches in glory by Christ Jesus" (Philippians 4:19). Furthermore we are surrounded by thousands of testimonies of God's ample provision for His people. I do not contend for the spirituality of a poverty syndrome; nor do I believe that "less is best," or that skimpiness is spiritual. I am confident that ". . . it is your Father's good pleasure to give you the kingdom" (Luke 12:32).

But it is most interesting to me that immediately after Jesus told us how much pleasure it gives the Father to share all He has with His children, Jesus added:

> Sell that ye have, and give alms; provide yourselves bags which wax not old, a treasure in the heavens that faileth not, where no thief approacheth, neither moth corrupteth. For where your treasure is, there will your heart be also.
>
> Luke 12:33, 34

Certainly there was nothing in the teaching of Jesus or any other New Testament writer that would authorize greed, love of luxury, or the acquiring of wealth. It is more a case of Father sharing with the older children so they can share with the younger.

When Jesus declared, "For where your treasure is, there will your heart be also" (Luke 12:34), He was establishing the principle of love investing itself in its object. If we love things, things will become the center of our lives. If we love people, we will become people centered. Oh, how today's church needs a theology that is both theocentric and Christocentric. We need to put God and Christ back as the core of our dreams, desires, fascination, and faith as a replacement of our self-centeredness.

The extreme emphasis of exercising faith for prosperity places man as the center of attention instead of God. It is "I, me, my, our" rather than God. It would seem that the whole purpose of faith was the acquisition of things rather than the revelation of God. The consistent emphasis on having anything that we confess ("name it, claim it") almost makes a divine genie of God who must do our bidding because we have rubbed the lamp of faith.

But God is not here for our convenience; we are here for His glory. Jesus did not come to earth as heaven's lawyer to settle an estate for men; He came as God's Lamb to settle the sin issue in men in order to return them to the relationship Adam enjoyed with God in the garden of Eden. There, Adam served God as the keeper of the garden and in giving love, communion, and fellowship to God in the cool of the day. Provision was there for Adam, but that provision was not the center of his life; God was.

When I move from the service of God and seek to employ God in my service, I have reversed the divine order. When I cease to accept God's provision for my life and seek to adjudicate what I will have, where I will go, how I will live, and how much of this world's goods I will possess, I am no longer acting as a child in my Father's care; I am usurping His prerogatives and evidencing a gross dissatisfaction with His will.

Those who make such indiscriminate use of Philippians 4:19, "But my God shall supply all your need according to his riches in glory by Christ Jesus," would do well to consider the context, for just a few verses earlier Paul had declared, "I know both how to be abased, and I know how to abound: every where and in all things I am instructed both to be full and to be hungry, both to abound and to suffer need" (Philippians 4:12). Paul willingly accepted all levels of God's provision for his life, fully aware that God would give him what was best for him at the time.

If, in fact, we could control the level of our prosperity by the exercise of our faith, we might very well create a situation that would lead to our departure from God. Consistently through the Old Testament, when Israel was allowed unlimited prosperity, she turned from God, but when God judged her with privation and captivity, she returned to the worship of Jehovah.

In Moses' great song setting forth the magnificent provisions of the Lord for His people he sang:

> But Jeshurun [a symbolic name for Israel] waxed fat, and kicked: thou art waxen fat, thou art grown thick, thou art covered with fatness; then he forsook God which made him, and lightly esteemed the Rock of his salvation. They provoked him to jealousy with strange gods, with abominations provoked they him to anger.
>
>   Deuteronomy 32:15, 16

Even the prophet Jeremiah cried on God's behalf, "I spake unto thee in thy prosperity; but thou saidst, I will not hear" (Jeremiah 22:21).

Even if prosperity were a friend of the Church, and history proves that it is not, the accompanying dangers need to be faced squarely. Israel learned dependence upon God by the provision of *daily* manna. At no time could she amass enough to become independent of God; still the human heart rebels at such continued dependence. In *Lectures on Hebrews*, S. Ridout reminds us that "All sin and all apostasy and departure from God begins when man loses his dependency upon God—man turns away from the Creator, and soon he knows not God."

Furthermore, if through the exercise of faith we do receive our hearts' desires, we must remember that we will be judged on our selection. When God appeared to Solomon in a dream and said, "... Ask what I shall give thee" (1 Kings 3:5), Solomon asked for a "listening heart" and wisdom to work God's kingdom.

> And the speech pleased the Lord, that Solomon had asked this thing. And God said unto him, Because thou hast asked this thing, and hast not asked for thyself long life; neither hast asked riches for thyself, nor hast asked the life of thine enemies; but hast asked for thyself understanding to discern judgment; Behold, I have done according to thy words: ... And I have also given thee that which thou hast not asked, both riches, and honour: so that there shall not be any among the kings like unto thee all thy days.
>
> 1 Kings 3:10–13

God was pleased that Solomon did *not* ask for the very things we are now being urged to exert faith for: possessions and positions. In the succeeding verses God pledges Solomon all the things that he did not ask for, and the Bible records that Solomon became wealthy beyond comparison of all kings before him or contemporary with him. But this was not the cry of his heart nor the area in which his faith was exercised; it was an addition for him. Jesus taught similarly when he declared, "But seek ye first the kingdom of God, and his righteousness; and all these things shall be added unto you" (Matthew 6:33). "Things" should be a by-product of our faith, never the main product of it. God and His kingdom must be the core of our desires, and out from that core will radiate such natural blessings as are needed in our lives. The will, way, and work of God are proper channels for our faith;

wealth, lavishness, and luxury are prostituted channels for our faith.

It is possible that God may give us our own way, but is it worth it? Some years ago I earnestly requested God for permission to leave the ministry and accept a business opportunity that had been placed before me. God agreed to release me, saying that I had already served in the ministry longer than He had required the Old Testament priests to serve. Furthermore, God promised to prosper me beyond anything I had ever experienced and assured me that the business would prosper. "But," He added, "with this you will have leanness of soul."

This devastated me, for I had seen others who had departed from God's perfect will for their lives to live according to their personal desires and watched that leanness of soul gnaw at them constantly. I withdrew my request, asked forgiveness for dissatisfaction with God's provisions, and have remained in the ministry for an additional twenty or more years, enjoying a fatness of soul which I judge to be far more valuable than a fat bank account.

Israel insisted on having her own way in the wilderness; "And he gave them their request; but sent leanness into their soul" (Psalms 106:15). With God's provision contentment and satisfaction follow, but when we determine the provision, they hasten to flee. How often does the possession of "things" seem to separate a person from happiness rather than bring it to him. Peace does not necessarily come with prosperity, but it always accompanies the presence of God.

In the prayer of Agur he petitions, "O God, I beg two favors from you before I die: First, help me never to tell a lie. Second, give me neither poverty nor riches! Give me just enough to satisfy my needs! For if I grow rich, I may become content without God. And if I am too poor, I may steal, and thus insult God's holy name" (Proverbs 30:7–9 LB). Wouldn't this be a safer position than predetermining what we "have a right to" and demanding it from God in the name of "faith"?

Irrespective of how we choose to channel our faith, we will be held accountable to God for our choices. If they were self-centered, we will be judged for selfishness. If they were God centered, we will be rewarded for obedience to His will. John writes, "And now, little children, abide in him; that, when he shall appear, we may have confidence, and not be ashamed before him at his coming" (1 John 2:28). "Abide in Him," not even abide in our faith. Our short span of life will soon be exhausted, and we will stand before God in the endlessness of eternity. The decision as to whether his discerning gaze will produce shame or joy in us must be made here and now.

If earthly joys are our immediate goal, we may be depriving ourselves of heavenly joys. If present possessions are the object of our faith, future positions with Christ may be forfeited, for Jesus Himself declared, ". . . It is easier for a camel to go through the eye of a needle, than for a rich man to enter into the kingdom of God" (Matthew 19:24).

It may be argued that our "confession" is the only thing that can limit our possession, and that "what you say is what you get," but, as one of the faith teachers likes to say, "You are hung by your tongue." Maybe there is more to confession than first meets the eye. Maybe confession that has self-interest as its center is more feigned faith than real.

23

Faith Versus Confession

Faith and confession are inseparably linked in the Scriptures. Both Jesus and Paul established this incontestably.

> And Jesus answering saith unto them, Have faith in God. For verily I say unto you, That whosoever *shall say* unto this mountain, Be thou removed, and be thou cast into the sea; and shall not doubt in his heart, but shall believe that those things *which he saith* shall come to pass; he shall have *whatsoever he saith.* Therefore I say unto you, What things soever ye desire, *when ye pray,* believe that ye receive them, and ye shall have them.
>
> Mark 11:22–24 (italics added)

It seems impossible to read this without an awareness that all our faith in God is revealed and released by the way we talk. It is not what we speculate but what we speak that produces action. Jesus was notable for the way He spoke His faith, for He spoke to the sea, and it immediately calmed. He spoke to a corpse, and life came to it instantly. He spoke to a tree, and it withered. So forceful and producing were the words of Jesus that Simon Peter declared, ". . . thou hast the words of eternal life" (John 6:68). Christ always spoke with the authority of the Eternal God.

Paul not only practiced an open, positive confession, he proclaimed it to others in writing:

> But what saith it? The word is nigh thee, *even in thy mouth,* and in thy heart: that is, the word of faith, which we

preach; That if thou shalt *confess with thy mouth* the Lord Jesus, and shalt believe in thine heart that God hath raised him from the dead, thou shalt be saved. For with the heart man believeth unto righteousness; and *with the mouth confession* is made unto salvation.

Romans 10:8–10 (italics added)

The obvious key to conversion is the confession of the Lordship of Jesus, not merely believing in our hearts. We must not only *see* Jesus as God's Christ; we must *say* what we see. We need to hear our mouth confess it; the demonic spirit world needs to be informed of our resignation; and God insists on hearing us confess His Son as our Lord and Savior.

Usually the word *confession* carries a negative connotation in religious circles. We are more apt to think of the confession of sin than the confession of righteousness, and this confession is valid and vital to Christian experience. But once sin has been confessed, it is cleansed (*see* 1 John 1:9), and we need no longer deal with that negative force. Christ dealt with it at Calvary. This leaves many Christians in a void or a vacuum as they retreat into their thought patterns wondering what the future holds for them. They have not been taught how to confess the Word of God as authoritative in their lives, nor have they fully grasped just who they are in Christ Jesus. Many continue to call themselves "only a sinner, saved by grace" long after the Scripture calls them saints in the making, sons in maturing, a church under construction, and a bride in preparation. Their lack of understanding, or their unwillingness to confess what God's Word says about them, keeps them from participating at a higher level with God.

Kenneth Hagin, in *How to Turn Your Faith Loose,* wrote:

> Christianity is called the great confession. What is confession? First, it's affirming something that we believe. Second, it's testifying to something that we know. Third, it's witnessing of a truth that we've embraced. Confession is affirming, testifying, and witnessing.
>
> We must know what we are to confess. Confession centers around five things. First, what God in Christ has wrought for us in the plan of redemption. Second, what God through the Word and the Holy Spirit has wrought in us in the new birth, and the infilling of the Holy Ghost. Third, what we are to God the Father in Christ Jesus. Fourth, what Jesus is doing for us now, at the right hand of the Father, where He ever liveth to make intercession for us. Fifth, what God can do through us, or what His Word will do through our lips.

None of us would argue with this definition and diagnosis of confession, for this is what God requires from each of us. What anemic ambassadors we would be if we could not correctly represent God in these five areas.

It is fundamental that there is no release of faith without confession, for it is our confession that gives expression to the faith we have received from God.

For this fresh emphasis of the truth of positive confession of our faith and speaking to the seemingly unsurmountable problems, the body of Christ is greatly indebted to the brothers who have toured this country teaching the faith message. The clear, concise command of Christ to speak to the mountain always brings a vigorous, vibrant hope back to the church, and this generation earnestly needs a renewed hope.

In every reemphasis of an abandoned truth new adherents tend to force the truth further than God's revelation, thereby bringing the church into error through overemphasis. One wonders which is better: error by underemphasis or error through overemphasis, for each is a deviation from the whole counsel of God. Still, deviation through overemphasis seems to frighten away honest seekers after truth far more than inaccuracy through underemphasis.

Embracing the faith teaching has caused many to swing the pendulum far too wide, and instead of bringing people into God's glorious liberty they have actually become bound in chains of frustration, introspection, and guilt. Because it is the needy who turn to God, the faith message has had a great application to human suffering and God's provision of healing. The sick have been told to confess their healing and function as though they were completely whole. If faith flows through that confession, then the healing will become a reality, but if God does not impart divine faith, no amount of confession will create it. Still the sick and infirm are told to confess their healing, ignore the symptoms, and keep both a positive attitude and a positive confession. If they fail in their confession, they are often put out of the church. Pastors have been dismissed from serving faith congregations just because a member of the household died. It was declared to be an evidence of a lack of faith.

If our confession created faith, then that form of theology might hold true. But confession only *releases* faith, it does not create faith. The success of ". . . he shall have whatsoever he saith" is dependent upon "Have faith in (or 'of ') God" (*see* Mark 11:22, 23). Until faith has been committed to us, it cannot be confessed by us. It is a dangerous oversimplification of truth to declare that *we* determine what we shall have by the words that we speak, and this simplistic theology leads to half-truths, disappointments, frustrations, and deep guilt.

Yet this concept of possessing creative power in our words is widely taught. By radio, television, conferences, and books we are informed that anything we desire is available to us if our concepts and confession are correct. This distortion of the words of Jesus denies sickness to any "true believer," fails to come to grips with death, chooses to ignore the dealings of God in the areas of privation, suffering, sickness, or accident. And all that is viewed by them as negative is conveniently attributed to the devil, while all that they define as good is ascribed to God.

That this simplistic dualism won't stand the test of the whole Bible doesn't seem to faze most of these disciples. Paul had to answer similar attitudes to the saints at Corinth. He wrote:

> Even unto this present hour we [apostles] both hunger, and thirst, and are naked, and are buffeted, and have no certain dwellingplace; And labour, working with our own hands: being reviled, we bless; being persecuted, we suffer it: Being defamed, we intreat: we are made as the filth of the world, and are the offscouring of all things unto this day.
>
> 1 Corinthians 4:11–13

Paul would undoubtedly have been put out of the faith fellowship. Nor would Jesus, who had no place to lay His head, have been a good example to many faith exponents. If Jesus ". . . learned . . . obedience by the things which he suffered," and was made ". . . perfect through sufferings" (Hebrews 5:8; 2:10) surely no amount of our confession can exempt us from similar dealings of God in our lives.

As Charles Farah, Jr., wrote in *From the Pinnacle of the Temple:* "Paul learned that although God wills health, we are not always healthy. He learned the secret not of total health but of total contentment (*see* Philippians 4:11). Paul clearly taught a Christian realism that admitted defeat when defeat had come, and hindrances when there had been hindrances."

It seems that this positive-confession teaching enjoins us to focus on our desires rather than on the higher purposes of God. Such self-centeredness is expected in infants, but maturity causes an adjustment to the will of the father (both in the natural and in the spiritual). "I delight to do thy will, O my God," David wrote (Psalms 40:8), and this is quoted concerning Christ in Hebrews 10:6–9. To confess what God wants for my life is one thing; to confess what I want for my life is quite another.

Joel Chandler Harris once said, "Watch out when you're getting all you want; fattening hogs ain't in luck." Still, any theology that puts creative power in the mouths of its adherents will be a popular theology, for it appeals to the American dream of affluence.

Yet, is the Bible message that I am the captain of my ship, the controller of my destiny, or is it that God, through Christ, is the sovereign Lord of my life? There is great insecurity in being totally in charge of our destiny, of knowing that one slip of the lip could bring sickness, accident, or financial ruin. It is far more comfortable to accept that "The angel of the Lord encampeth round about them that fear him, and delivereth them" (Psalms 34:7) than to have to combat the powers of hell, poverty, sickness, and disaster with our positive confession.

Granted that the church has underplayed her authority in Christ, but is it justifiable to overstate her authority? Can't we come back into balance as believers and return God to His creative throne and become His dependent children, gladly confessing what He has said to us and done for us? If the eleventh chapter of Hebrews is, indeed, the model of how faith works, we must recognize that before it speaks of the working faith of Abel, Enoch, Noah, and others, it declares "Through faith we understand that the worlds were framed by the word of God. . ." (Hebrews 11:3). The first step in faith is dependence upon God. He, not we, is the creator. We submit to Him, not He to us. He speaks into existence; we can only say what He says.

Positive confession? Yes! But not to create faith, for faith has its origins in God Himself. The purpose of positive confession is to release faith to the problem or circumstance—to say to the situation what God has said to us. This may give us God's power of attorney, but it doesn't make gods out of us. Our authority is totally delegated; our power is conferred, and our faith has been received. We produce none of it; we only proclaim it.

Does this positive confession for whatever we want really work? Sometimes, and for some persons, it seems to. But, as evangelist Jed Smock said at a recent conference, "A lot of what is passing for faith today is nothing but big talk." Much of the success of "positive confession for things" is due more to a vast mailing list, radio and television audiences, or massive convention attendance than it is to faith. It is feigned faith, pure and simple.

Perhaps the most dangerous aspect of positive-confession teaching is that it walks a narrow borderline between faith and metaphysics. Many who have never accepted Christ as their Savior have made similar principles work in their lives. Where do we step from divine to demonic function?

24
Faith Versus Metaphysics

Dr. Ernest Holmes, in his book *Science of Mind,* says, "The idea that faith has only to do with our religious experience, is a mistake. Faith is a faculty of the mind that finds its highest expression in the religious attitude.... Those who have great faith have great power. Faith is an affirmative, mental approach to reality."

It may come as a surprise to many earnest Christians that all of the "mental sciences" embrace faith as a fundamental force. Not only does the Eternal God of Heaven and Earth work on a faith principle, the "god of this world" (*see* 2 Corinthians 4:4) also works on a principle of faith, for faith is a necessary bridge between the natural and the spiritual world.

In speaking of faith versus metaphysics I am using *Merriam-Webster's* definition of metaphysics: 1(b) "the more abstruse philosophical sciences" rather than as the name of a religious system. The mind sciences, whether they be philosophy, Theosophy, Christian Science, Metaphysics, Unity, or the many other titles that are used, are all great proponents of faith. They emphasize the power of the mind and often define this power as "faith."

A few years ago on a conference ground in California Dr. James A. Hershey asked for an audience with me, during which he gave me his testimony. He had spent his lifetime as a pastor or practitioner in many of the mind-science groups, progressing from one to the other in his search for satisfaction in his soul and spirit. In the mercy of God, and through the consistent testimony of an evangelist who used to be in the mind sciences, Dr. Hershey finally met Jesus, and although he was Jewish, he embraced Him as the Lord Jesus Christ. After hearing his testimony, I encouraged him to write it, and for the following year I worked with him to get it into book form. Unfortunately, he died before the work was completed.

During the months that we visited, wrote, and phoned each other, we were both impressed with the similarity between some of what is being propounded as "faith teaching" and the very darkness out of which Dr. Hershey had been saved. Repeatedly he would tell me, "I used to preach that when I was pastoring mental-science churches." Dr. Hershey told me of the successes he had achieved by the exercise of "mind power" and the discipline of positive thinking. Over and over he urged me to warn present-day Christians to beware of going beyond the clear teaching of the Word of God, for the moment we proceed beyond God's boundaries we are open to the instruction of "the angel of light" (*see* 2 Corinthians 11:14).

To the churches that invited him to give his testimony he declared, "Satan brings eight points of truth to bring two lies. When a person proves the eight points, he automatically accepts the two lies as truth also, and doesn't question them." He also used to warn that, "humanistic psychology, where man starts from himself rather than from the God of the Bible, leads man to despair and has no meaning. It has no absolutes, and every man does his own thing."

He admitted, "I was wrapped up in self, yet I was loving and kind; at least I thought I was. I kept planting my seeds of faith, saying positive affirmations that caused people to believe in me. I was convinced that I could have as much as I could believe for, and this I taught in my classes. I put on a good front talking positively, enthusiastically, optimistically, and faith-filledly, but my life was a mess. I had no peace, my marriage was ruined, and I kept getting disillusioned as I got deeper and deeper into these philosophies."

He told me, "One thing that I discovered early in my lecturing across the country, and then in my ministry, disturbed me. Many of the people coming to my 'ministry' were not God fearing or even God believing. There were board members or parishioners who merely wanted to use the Mind Science to bring great wealth and success in the business world and in the material world. They really didn't believe in God or anything spiritual, but they liked the idea that right thinking—abundant thinking—brought abundance and success."

Dr. Hershey reminded me that the top businesses in our country hire experts, often at very fancy dollar figures, to conduct seminars teaching these principles of affirmation, believing in yourself, exuding self-confidence, the "I can" philosophy, being optimistic, setting goals, and positive confession. He used to direct such seminars. In our conversations together he would often compare some "faith rallies" we had attended with some of these seminars he used to conduct and said that the fundamental difference he could see was that the "faith rally" had used the name of God and Scripture verses as proof texts. Otherwise it was basically the same philosophy he had used in the business seminars and in his classes in metaphysics.

This, of course, must be balanced with what has already been written. I am not bringing a wholesale indictment against the faith teaching, but I am asking that we take a close look at a few of the extreme positions some disciples,

and a few teachers, have taken in this matter. That they may
have gone beyond the whole counsel of God doesn't seem to
bother them too much for, as one of their writers, Frederic K.
C. Price, declared, "The church has been satisfied to feed on
the *dry husks of philosophy* and to eat at the *slop-tray of theology*.
Consequently the church has not known its rights, and the
devil has lorded it over us." If they view theology as a "slop-
tray," then we're all in trouble, for, according to *Webster's
Dictionary,* theology is "rational interpretation of religious
faith, practice, and experience; *specifically:* a branch of systematic theology dealing with God and his relation to the
world." If rational interpretation of our faith and practice
and the systematic study of God is "slop-tray," then what is
the philosophy and ideology that is being taught in the name
of God?

When pressed to undergird their extreme teachings on
faith, a common defense is, "It works, and you can't argue
with success." But Dr. Ernest Holmes wrote, "It seems when
we are dealing with Metaphysics that we are dealing with
something too abstract. But what is more tangible than results?"

Are results sufficient proof of correctness of belief? Can the
end justify the means? I can remember that in the classroom
getting the right answer was only part of the process. I also
had to show a right computation, for the correct sum
improperly computed was still considered to be a wrong answer. Is it possible to obtain the desired results by the wrong
means? Could we, in the name of faith, be laying hold of
psychic power, or even worse, a demonic force?

Faith teaching demands a positive attitude and confession
at all times, and says that what is proclaimed will be possessed. The business world teaches the same thing under the
title of "positive thinking," and the mental sciences claim

that what we can conceive we can receive; that life is a mirror, and what we put in front of the mirror is what we receive.

Ernest Holmes, the founder of one system of Metaphysics, says, "Our creative mind cannot stop creating. What we place there makes all the difference in the world. So the words we use, how we say them (with feeling) as well as our thoughts, can be very creative and good or destructive and bad."

Faith teaching beautifully emphasizes the believer's position in Christ Jesus, but it declares that out of that positional authority comes conditional authority: that as "sons of God" we function in the authority of God, even to the point of commanding God. In comparison, Dr. Holmes writes, "There is in every individual that which partakes of the Universal wholeness—and in so far as it operates—it is God. That is the meaning of the word *Emmanuel*—the meaning of the word *Christ*. That Universal wholeness—God—reacts to us according to our belief in it. *It is done to each of us as we believe.*" Being positioned in Christ is one thing; taking the position of Christ is quite another. Dr. Hershey used to remind me, "Mental Science doesn't deny the divinity of Christ—it affirms the divinity of all people."

Receiving and acting on God's promises is commendable, but trying to force God to react to our commands just because we have recited the correct words or phrases smacks of magic more than faith. God may have "raised us up together, and made us sit together in heavenly places in Christ Jesus" (Ephesians 2:6), but this does not make miniature "Christ Jesuses" out of us. He is still the King; we are His kids. We participate in His gifts and provisions, but we do not produce them by our attitudes and words. He is the sovereign God; we are the suppliant guests.

Another questionable teaching of some of the "faith teachers" is that all symptoms must be ignored and declared to be
lies of the devil. Just how does this differ from the mental sciences? Dr. Holmes said, "The Practitioner, in order to be
sure his treatment works, must first deny what his senses tell
him, whether it be disease, limitation, confusion, fear, evil.
He must keep denying and then affirm what he knows to be
'really' true in the mind of God. Then he 'realizes' the truth
and declares it. Then he 'knows' his treatment is successful."

I have counseled people who bore the heavy load of guilt
for the death of a loved one simply because during a pro-
longed illness they had mentioned how sick the loved one
seemed to be. Their faith doctrine placed upon them the responsibility for the death, for, as they told me, had they
maintained a positive confession and had not acknowledged
the sickness, their loved one would have gotten well.

Any faith that cannot come to grips with reality is not a
Bible faith. Daniel did not deny the reality of the lions or his
precarious position with them in the den, but his faith preserved him in the midst of it. Jesus never denied the reality
of sickness, disease, or death, but His divine faith overcame it
beautifully. Faith that demands a hypnotic denial of the existence of negative factors in our lives is more cultic than
Christian.

Dr. Hershey told me, "All mental sciences believe that suffering is not necessary. All men need to do is awaken in understanding of God's laws; live in accordance with them, and
all suffering will cease." We seem to hear a similar philosophy being taught as though it came out of the Bible. In the
name of faith there is an embracing of escapism from the
dealings of God, yet David admitted, ". . . thou hast enlarged me when I was in distress . . ." (Psalms 4:1). If we
could, by an exercise of proclamation, prevent God's deal-

ings in our lives, and, praise the Lord, we can't, we would stunt our spiritual growth and remain small-souled Christians.

It may be argued that mind sciences have developed their basic doctrines of faith from the Scriptures and that is why there is so much similarity to present-day faith teaching. Although I know that each counterfeit must have a real counterpart, I am also aware that it often requires an expert to tell them apart.

Is faith really an exercise of mind over matter, or is it a divine impartation that really matters? Does faith change our attestation or our attainment? Faith, as Jesus spoke of it, should change our circumstance, not merely our confession; it should affect crisis situations, not merely Christian speech.

While I do not charge that the faith teachers are unwitting practitioners of the mind sciences, I am advocating a return to the clear, concise, consecutive teaching of the whole Word of God as the only safe source of teaching on faith that works. God hates mixture, as is evidenced in the Law's prohibition of yoking two different kinds of animals together, or the weaving of wool and flax together in a garment. Perhaps if we will return to the pure, simple, divine faith of the Scriptures, we will have more results and less recrimination, and we can move from feigned faith to unfeigned faith.

Because these extreme positions on faith cannot and will not consistently work, there are many former adherents of faith who could not make it work for them and who have abandoned the whole scheme of faith, even saving faith. They have become apostates. Look with me at the steps in apostasy.

25
Faith Versus Apostasy

Those who search for apparent contradictions in the Bible enjoy pointing out two conflicting verses in the writings of Paul. To the church at Rome Paul declared "... God hath dealt to every man the measure of faith" (Romans 12:3), but to the church in Thessalonica Paul said, "... for all men have not faith" (2 Thessalonians 3:2). This is not a contradiction; it is a comparison. It is true that in the mercy of God all men have had a measure of faith dealt to them, but it is equally true that many of them have not nurtured and maintained this faith. The world has always had an abundance of Hymenaeuses and Alexanders who "concerning faith have made shipwreck" (*see* 1 Timothy 1:19, 20).

None has ever been destroyed by God's faith, for God's faith brings life, not death. But many who began in faith ended in *apostasy,* a word that means "renunciation of a religious faith (or) defection." That which they once revered, they renounced; they defected from that in which they once delighted. Faith became a fallacy for them. They once relied on faith, but now they rebel at it. They have become apostate to the faith.

Some have abandoned the very truth in which they abode because they never found unfeigned faith—true, divine faith. They had embraced a pseudofaith—a feigned faith—a doctrinal concept—without a divine commitment, and when they could not make it work for them they deserted it.

Theirs was a conscious, deliberate forsaking of something that proved to be false.

But a great number of people get involved in apostasy even after they have been partakers of and participants in God's true, unfeigned faith. Usually their recantation is subtle and is more a work of their subconscious than their conscious minds. It is seldom a deliberate renunciation of faith; it is more likely an insidious replacement of that faith.

In Paul's first letter to Timothy he lists five ways people who have once walked in faith end up bankrupt of faith.

First, he writes, "Now the Spirit speaketh expressly, that in the latter times some shall *depart* from the faith . . ." (1 Timothy 4:1, italics added), and then he lists as the reason for their departure: (1) heeding seducing spirits; (2) observing doctrines of devils; (3) deceitful hypocrisy; (4) prohibiting marriage; and (5) prohibition of eating certain foods (*see* 1 Timothy 4:1–3). Certainly we have seen that undue concern with the demonic has caused some to depart from the faith, and undue asceticism in the matter of marriage or foods eaten does not deepen our faith; it causes a departure from faith. The issue seems to be that these individuals have allowed themselves to get caught up in and centered in something short of God, who alone is ". . . the author and finisher of our faith . . ." (Hebrews 12:2).

Second, Paul tells Timothy, "But if any provide not for his own, and specially for those of his own house, he hath *denied* the faith, and is worse than an infidel" (1 Timothy 5:8, italics added). Denial of the faith, as Paul sees it, is not a negative confession but an unwillingness to provide support for the family. For the past few years there has been a high incidence of individuals who wanted to "live by faith," which often turned out to be little more than bumming a living off

the church. Refusing to work so one can have more time for
Bible reading and prayer is not living by faith; it is *denial* of
faith. In my book *Let Us Abide* I write:

> When Paul wrote his epistle to the church at Thessalon-
> ica, he found it necessary to say: "But we beseech you,
> brethren ... that ye *study* (Greek, 'be ambitious') to be
> quiet, and to *do your own business,* and *to work with your own
> hands,* as we have commanded you; That ye may walk
> honestly toward them that are without, and *that ye have lack
> of nothing"* (*see* 1 Thessalonians 4:10–12, italics added). It
> would seem that even in his day there were some who had
> to be admonished to go to work. I guess that the concept
> that the world owes us a living isn't so new after all. Lazi-
> ness is inherent in most of our natures, and unless we con-
> quer it, it will control us. In a day when welfare, unem-
> ployment payments, disability insurance, and guaranteed
> income are so available, the lazy man can make a career of
> doing nothing and depending upon society to provide for
> him ... But the Bible does not make society responsible for
> the lazy and indigent. It merely offers work for the able
> and aid for the poor.

Third, Paul speaks of those who ". . . have *cast off* their first
faith" (1 Timothy 5:12, italics added) declaring this will
happen when "the younger widows ... have begun to wax
wanton against Christ ..." (v. 11). The expression "wax
wanton" refers to passion or sensual desires. How Satan likes
to stir inordinate sexual desire in the faithful believers, for he
well knows the power this drive exerts on the human nature.
The first group *departed* from the faith in forbidding marriage; this group has *cast off* their faith to embrace sensual
pleasure. Any time sensual desire is given expression outside

the channels of marriage, it will be such an enemy to our
faith that we will either cast off our immorality or we must
cast off our faith. Impurity of life is an antithesis to a life of
faith; it wars against that faith and sets itself on a course to
destroy that faith. The amoral attitude America is taking toward sex is already causing many to *cast off* their faith. Oh,
they may not cease to attend church; quite the contrary, for
we now have special churches for those living in open immorality. But there will be no unfeigned faith among them,
since in order to embrace an unscriptural sex life they had to
release their faith in the inspired Word of God and in the
claims of the God of that inspiration. It is a flinging to the
winds of a faith in order to have a fling in sensuality. What
price pleasure!

Fourth, Paul says, "For some are already *turned aside* after
Satan" (1 Timothy 5:15). Interestingly enough the context
does not speak of witchcraft or Satan worship; it talks about
idleness, gossiping, talebearing, and busybody activity. This,
the Spirit says, is demonic activity. Paul's answer to this was
to urge marriage, the bearing of children, and proper care of
the house. Idleness becomes the spawning ground for much
mischief. While our society is clamoring for more and more
free time, it is also *turning aside* from faith. In many recre-
ational areas pastors secretly rejoice at inclement weather on
Sunday, for it usually means a larger attendance at the Sunday services inasmuch as there is nowhere else to go in a
rainstorm.

How many who have embraced faith in poverty have
turned aside from it in plenty! And any pastor could give
you names of people who turned to God's unfeigned faith in
a time of desperate illness but who turned aside from it when
they regained their health. It is not so much that God is un-

desirable; it is that other things become even more desirable. When it is a choice between God's faith and man's fun, the faith generally gets turned aside.

Fifth, Paul speaks of two groups who have *erred from the faith (see* 1 Timothy 6:10; 21). The first group erred from the faith in covetousness over money. Love of money and materialism have caused many to err from the faith, and, as Paul adds, "pierced themselves through with many sorrows" (v.10). If a love for things is the occasion for many sorrows and an occasion to err from the faith, what a shame that this is set forth as a motivating force to get people interested in faith in the first place. They are promised whatever they can believe for, but when their lust levels rise, they find that they have "wandered away from the faith," as many modern translations put it. While using faith to get things, they wandered away from the faith, leaving them with the love of money and hearts broken with many sorrows.

The second group erred or wandered from the faith through intellectualism. Paul's warning was, "Timothy, guard what has been entrusted to your care. Turn away from godless chatter and the opposing ideas of what is falsely called knowledge, which some have professed and in so doing have wandered from the faith" (1 Timothy 6:20, 21 NIV). Godless talk and foolish arguments with those who boast of their knowledge can sidetrack us from really knowing God, which is the ultimate purpose of faith.

There is no question that "God hath dealt to every man the measure of faith" (Romans 12:3) for natural life would be seriously impaired without it, and salvation is impossible without it, but not all men have faith. Some have *departed* from the faith; others have *denied* the faith; still others have *cast off, turned aside,* and *erred or wandered* from the faith that was given to them. In every instance their loss of faith was the result of a positive action or attitude: refusal to work, lust, idleness, materialism, or intellectualism. It was never a direct refutation of that faith; it was a replacement of that faith with something else. Maintaining faith requires maturing in our relationship with God. Anything that replaces that relationship also replaces our faith.

Can anyone live in a decadent society such as ours and maintain the level of faith that God committed to him? Noah did; Abraham did; Lot did; and Moses did. They lived in evil times with far less light than we possess, yet the eleventh chapter of Hebrews showed them, and many others, maintaining their faith in God and the promises of God in the midst of circumstances worse than we face. The secret seems to be their intimate relationship with God. They did not increase their faith by planting it like a seed, but by praying to God. They did not maintain their faith through works, but through worship. They didn't spend their days claiming the promises, but in celebrating the Promiser.

It is likely that unless we return to their values and emulate their actions, we may end up in unmitigated apostasy rather than unfeigned faith. Peter declares that we ". . . have obtained like precious faith . . . through the righteousness of God and our Saviour Jesus Christ" (2 Peter 1:1). God grant us such a warmth of relationship with Himself that we will never obscure this precious faith we have obtained from Him.

We can be apostolic in our faith or apostate to that faith, depending upon whether we willingly move in unfeigned faith or feigned faith, on whether we embrace the correlatives to faith or the contrarieties to faith. God's faith is precious and pure when we receive it; any pollutants that are added must come from us.

Postlude
Living by Faith

It's time to go. The message is over, and the service is through, but may we leave with the stirring strains of the postlude.

The minor prophet Habakkuk, standing in his watch-tower, was granted a vision involving the end times. In this divine visitation he was told, ". . . the just shall live by his faith" (Habakkuk 2:4), and following the vision he offered a prayer that was to be sung to a double harp, so great was the excitement of this revelation.

When God quickened this truth to the heart of a Roman Catholic priest named Martin Luther, it became the touch-stone of the Reformation—*the just shall live by faith*. It is not merely that those whom Christ has justified shall be posses-sors of faith, but their lives will be lives of faith. Faith, there-fore, becomes more than a force; it is a focus. Faith is far more than a channel through which we receive gifts; it is a calling in which we respond to God. We live, not lust, by faith. Faith is far more a walk than a work; it is a way of liv-ing that is assured in the Old Testament and reassured three times in the New Testament.

"For therein is the righteousness of God revealed *from* faith *to* faith: as it is written, The just shall live by faith," Paul wrote (Romans 1:17, italics added). In this letter the em-phasis in the context is on "the just." Not all shall live by faith, but "the just," those who have accepted the finished work of Christ Jesus as efficacious for their sins, shall "live by faith." What began as a work of faith will be lived out as a work of faith. The process is "from faith to faith." It is progressive and continuous; past and contemporary. He who declared us "just" has decreed a life of faith. They are supposed to go together like bread and butter.

To the church in Galatia that was striving with legalism and works of the law Paul wrote, "But that no man is justified by the law in the sight of God, it is evident: for, The just shall live by faith" (Galatians 3:11). In quoting Habakkuk in this letter Paul seems to emphasize "shall live." Earlier Paul had told them, "I live by the faith of the Son of God, who loved me, and gave himself for me" (*see* Galatians 2:20); now he is enjoining them to stop trying to live by the law and learn to live by God's faith.

In *Let Us Abide* I wrote:

> The life of faith is not optional; it is obligatory. It was never offered as an elective for the supersaints. It is not a matter of preference; it is a prerequisite to divine life. Therefore, great portions of the Old Testament are devoted to revealing, often in painstaking detail, the steps God used to develop a life and walk of faith in His men.

It is God's will that we *"live* by faith," not merely subsist by faith. Inasmuch as Jesus declared, ". . . I am come that they might have life, and that they might have it more abundantly" (John 10:10), we gather that to *live* by faith is to live abundantly, with nothing needful lacking. It is to enjoy emotional stability, financial security, and, most of all, spiritual satisfaction. What a way to live!

Just before beginning the flamboyant faith chapter, the writer to the Hebrews said, "Now the just shall live by faith: but if any man draw back, my soul shall have no pleasure in him" (Hebrews 10:38). This time as the Holy Spirit quotes Habakkuk, he seems to put the emphasis upon "faith," for He follows it with a warning against apostasy—drawing back. The life that the "just one" shall live is a life of *faith.*

Quoting again from *Let Us Abide,* I said:

> In the epistles of the New Testament . . . we find at least sixteen areas of divine grace available to us through faith. For faith is listed as the source of, or channel for our: access to grace, healing, indwelling of Christ, justification, life, promise of the Spirit, propitiation, protection (shield and breastplate), righteousness, salvation, sanctification, standing, strength, steadfastness, understanding, and walk.

With all this available to us through faith, it is no wonder at all that he who lives the life of faith lives an abundant life. Why live at a level beneath the life of faith, when it is both easier and better to live by faith? As J. Gresham Machen puts it, "Faith means not doing something but receiving something; it means not the earning of a reward but the acceptance of a gift."

Living by faith does not mean doing without, or not doing at all; it means *doing His will.* It is a walking with God into new territory as Abraham did. It is obeying God when the request seems incongruous to all known facts, as in Noah's life. It is learning to depend rather than developing independence.

Because of the many unknown variables, living by faith can present its own set of insecurities. As Joe Garlington said in a recent conference, "A life of faith is like walking a precipice while surrounded by a miracle." There are risks to living by faith, but the rewards far outweigh any risks. The key to success is to always keep Christ Jesus as the object of our faith. He has never failed.